IMPORTANT NOTICE

The Forest Service has renumbered all of the forest roads in Western Washington.

The old numbering system was derived over thirty years ago, before road planners had any indication of the maze of roads that would eventually be developed. The new numbering system should make road directions easier to follow.

Unfortunately, most maps still use the old numbers. For many hikes we have listed the old and new numbers side by side, so that old maps and new road signs can be used together.

100 Hikes in the

Alpine Lakes

**Text: Vicky Spring, Ira Spring,
and Harvey Manning
Photos: Bob and Ira Spring,
Kirkendall/Spring**

The Mountaineers
Seattle

THE MOUNTAINEERS: Organized ████ ████ ████ udy, preserve and enjoy the natural beauty of the Northwest."

Published by The Mountaineers, 306 Second Avenue West
Seattle, Washington 98119

Published simultaneously in Canada by Douglas & McIntyre, Ltd.
1615 Venables Street, Vancouver, British Columbia V5L 2H1

Manufactured in the United States of America

Edited by Barbara Chasan
Designed by Marge Mueller; maps by Helen Sherman, Gary Rands,
    and Judith Siegel
Cover: Lila Lake and Box Ridge, Alpine Lakes region
Frontispiece: Lake Viviane and McClellan Peak, Enchantment Lakes region

Library of Congress Cataloging in Publication Data

Spring, Vicky, 1953–
    100 hikes in the Alpine Lakes.

    Includes index.
    1. Hiking—Washington (State)—Alpine Lakes
Wilderness—Guide-books. 2. Alpine Lakes Wilderness
(Wash.)—Guide-books. I. Spring, Ira. II. Manning,
Harvey. III. Title. IV. One hundred hikes in the Alpine
Lakes.
GV199.42.W22A477   1985   917.97   85-18849
ISBN 0-89886-108-X

0   9   8   7   6

5   4   3   2

CONTENTS

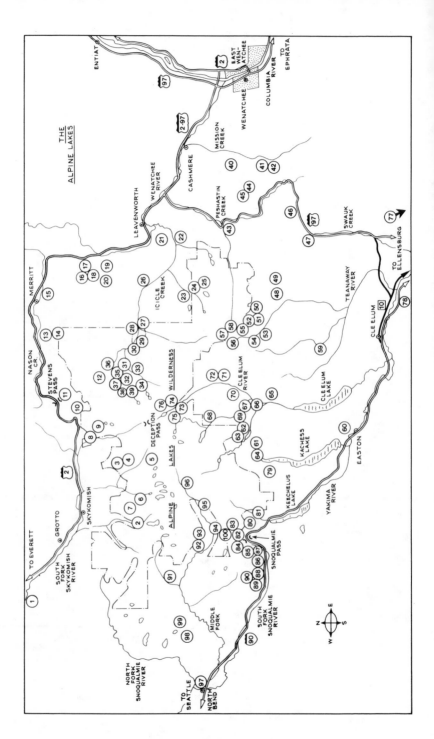

THE
ALPINE LAKES

Location	Page	Status

8

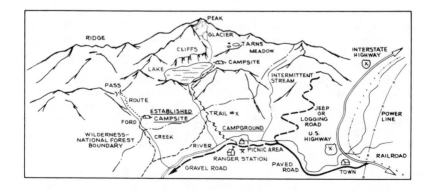

SAVING OUR TRAILS

Preservation Goals for the 1980s and Beyond

In the early 1960s The Mountaineers began publishing trail guides as another means of working "to preserve the natural beauty of Northwest America," through putting more feet on certain trails, in certain wildlands. We suffered no delusion that large numbers of boots improve trails or enhance wildness. However, we had learned to our rue that "you use it or lose it," that threatened areas could only be saved if they were more widely known and treasured. We were criticized in certain quarters for contributing to the deterioration of wilderness by publicizing it, and confessed the fault, but could only respond, "Which would you prefer? A hundred boots in a virgin forest? Or that many snarling wheels in a clearcut?"

As the numbers of wilderness lovers have grown so large as to endanger the qualities they love, the rules of "walking light" and "camping no trace" must be the more faithfully observed. Yet the ultimate menace to natural beauty is not hikers, no matter how destructive their great, vicious boots may be, nor even how polluting their millions of *giardia* cysts, but doomsday, arriving on two or three or four or six or eight wheels, or on tractor treads, or on whirling wings—the total conquest of the land and water and sky by machinery.

Victories Past

Conceived in campfire conversations of the 1880s, Olympic National Park was established in 1938, the grandest accomplishment of our most conservation-minded president, Franklin D. Roosevelt. (Confined to a wheelchair and never himself able to know the trails with his own feet, FDR nevertheless saw the fallacy in the sneering definition of wilderness as "preserves for the aristocracy of the physically fit," knew the value of dreams that never could be personally attained.)

A renewal of the campaigns after World War II brought—regionally, in 1960—the Glacier Peak Wilderness and—nationally, in 1964—the Wilderness Act whereby existing and future wildernesses were placed beyond the fickleness of bureaucracies, guarded by Congress and the President against thoughtless tampering.

1968 was the year of the North Cascades Act, achieving another vision of the nineteenth century, the North Cascades National Park, plus the Lake Chelan and Ross Lake National Recreation Areas, Pasayten Wilderness, and additions to the Glacier Peak Wilderness.

In 1976 the legions of citizens laboring at the grass roots, aided by the matching dedication of certain of their Congressmen and Senators, obtained the Alpine Lakes Wilderness.

In 1984 the same alliance, working at the top and at the bottom and all through the middle, all across the state, won the Washington Wilderness Act, encompassing more than 1,000,000 acres.

Is, therefore, the job done?

Goals Ahead

Absolutely not.

Had hikers been content with the victory of 1938 there never would have been those of 1960, 1968, 1976, and 1984. The American nation as a whole has a step or two yet to go before attaining that condition of flawless perfection where it fits seamlessly into the final mosaic of the Infinite Plan, and the same is true of the National Wilderness Preservation System.

Companion volumes to this, covering the North Cascades and the South Cascades and Olympics, note major omissions. The area of this book was not addressed by the 1984 Act because of the recency of the 1976 Act establishing the Alpine Lakes Wilderness. However, this is not to say 1976 was the end of the Alpine Lakes story. Very sizable areas all around the wilderness were recognized as "belonging" in it, but because of private ownership dating from the Northern Pacific Land Grant of 1864, could not be immediately included. The present highest priority is obtaining these private lands, preferably by purchase, but in the current status of national finances, most probably by land exchange. Among the current chief goals are obtaining Icicle Ridge, from the edge of Leavenworth to the highlands of Ladies Pass country; lands in and around Tumwater Canyon; approaches to the region of McCue Ridge and Chiwaukum Creek; the Pratt River, draining to the Middle Fork Snoqualmie River; and the checkerboard of the Teanaway River and the ridge from Blewett Pass to Ingalls Peak. There further are matters of management in the adjoining lands, outside the wilderness, such as the apparent intention of the Forest Service to convert the entire east slope of the Cascades to motorcycle Heaven (pedestrian Hell).

However, it needs to be kept uppermost in mind that designation as "wilderness" or "national park" or "national whatever" is a means, not the end. The goals ahead are not words on a document or lines on a map but the protection of the land these symbols may signify. Any other symbols that do the job are satisfactory. The *protection* is the thing.

In contrast to the immediate past, the preservationist agenda of the immediate future is focused less on redrawing the maps than employing any practical method to preserve roadless areas from further invasion by machinery. In fact, we are now at a stage where the saving of trails, important though that is, has a lower priority than the saving of fisheries and wildlife resources, scientific values, gene pools, and another contribution of wildland too long neglected, the provision of dependable and pure water for domestic and agricultural needs.

What In the World Happened To Us?

The wheel is more than the symbol. It is the fact. The National Wilderness Act so recognizes by banning "mechanized travel," including *but not limited to* motorized travel; bicycles—"mountain bikes"—are excluded too, for the simple reason that in appropriate terrain they readily can go 5–10 miles per hour, an "unnatural" speed often incompatible with the "natural" 1–3 miles per hour of the traveler on foot.

Outside the boundaries of dedicated wilderness, many trails can be amicably shared by bicycles and pedestrians, both capable of being quiet and minimally destructive and disruptive of the backcountry scene. Attach a motor to the wheels, however, and the route no longer deserves to be called a "trail," it becomes a *road*.

In the past quarter-century conservationists have been busy saving Washington trails by creating a new national park and a bouquet of new wildernesses. Meanwhile, officials of the U.S. Forest Service have been assiduously converting *true trails* (that is, paths suitable for speeds of perhaps up to 5 or so miles per hour, the pace of a horse) to *motorcycle roads* (that is, "trails" built to let the off-road vehicle—the ORV—do 15–30 miles per hour).

In this quarter-century the concerted efforts of tens of thousands of conservationists protected large expanses of wildland from invasion by machines—but during the same period a comparative handful of ORVers have taken away more miles of trails, converting them to de facto roads, than the conservationists have saved. As the score stands in 1985, only 45 percent of Washington trails are machine-free—in national parks and wildernesses; of the other 55 percent, half are open to motorcycles—and thus are not truly trails at all.

When automobiles arrived in America the citizenry and government were quick to see they should not be permitted on sidewalks. The Forest Service (and let it be added, the Washington State Department of Natural Resources, or DNR) is slower to recognize that whenever there are more than a few scattered travelers of either kind the differences in speed and purpose between motorized wheels and muscle-powered feet are irreconcilable.

Thinking to serve the laudable purpose of supplying "a wide spectrum of recreational opportunities," the Forest Service initially tolerated ORVs, then began encouraging them, widening and straightening and smoothing "multiple-use trails" to permit higher speeds, thus increasing the number of motors and discouraging hikers, in the end creating "single-purpose ORV trails"—in a word, roads.

Federal funds were employed for the conversion until that source dried up; since 1979 the Forest Service has relied heavily on money from the State of Washington Interagency for Outdoor Recreation (IAC), the subject of the following section of this book. Perhaps the most pernicious result is not the environmental damage, much of which can be repaired in time, but the appalling fact that when it accepts IAC funds the Forest Service signs a contract guaranteeing the trail or the equivalent to be kept open for ORVs in perpetuity. "Forever" surely is a major land-use decision, yet these conversions are made without environmental assessment, with only token public hearings, the notices tucked away in the fine print of small community newspapers.

Certainly, the Forest Service could not engage in such large-scale, long-term conversion of trails to roads if hikers were given the respect their numbers—overwhelming compared to the motorcyclists—deserve.

Hikers spoke up for the Washington Wilderness Act of 1984. By the many thousands they wrote letters to congressmen and senators. The pen is mightier than the wheel, and it must be taken up again, by those same tens of thousands, to write letters to congressmen and senators, with copies to the Regional Forester, Region 6, U.S.F.S., 319 S.W. Pine Street,

P.O. Box 3623, Portland, Oregon 97208, asking that:

1. Trails be considered a valuable resource, treated as a separate category in all Forest Plans.

2. All trail users should be notified of public meetings concerning any Forest Plan affecting trails; public meetings should be held in metropolitan areas as well as in small, remote communities near the trails.

3. To help reduce the conflict between hikers and ORVs, hikers on multiple-use trails (often with little children and heavy packs) shall have the right of way when meeting motors. For the safety of both parties, a speed limit of 7 mph shall be enforced on all multiple-use trails.

We do not concede that a "multiple-use trail" is a trail at all, but these measures can help ameliorate the present danger, until philosophical retraining of land managers can be accomplished.

Harvey Manning

OF FEET AND WHEELS AND MONEY

Trails are becoming an endangered species. In 1946, the year I started working as a full-time photographer, there were 144,060 miles of trails in the United States and only 107,731 miles of roads. However, by 1983 trails had decreased 32 percent, to 98,825 miles, and roads had increased 300 percent, to 321,000 miles.[1]

As the number of hikers in the Northwest and the nation has grown, the number of trails has steadily declined. Hikers have already lost 32 percent of the trails to road building; to accommodate future logging, the Forest Service may very well destroy another 10 to 20 percent in the next 10 years. Another 30 percent[2] is jeopardized by the Forest Service's dedication to "a wide spectrum of recreational opportunities"—that is, rough "multiple-use trails" that had been used by an occasional motorcyclist are now being improved to encourage motorcycles. In some areas trails are already so heavily used by motorcycles that hikers no longer use them. If the Forest Service continues to encourage ORV use by converting trails to motorcycle standards, hikers will be displaced from most of the multiple-use trails.

Hikers cannot expect to entirely rid the trails of ORVs and motorcycles, certainly not in the immediate future; they have become too entrenched in the past 20 years. However, if hikers will speak out, their proliferation can be stopped. Hikers should ask their congressmen three questions: (1) Should motorcycles be on trails? (2) Are motorcyclists in conflict with other users? (3) Do we have enough space and money to accommodate ORVs on trails? The first two relate to philosophical policies the Forest Service has heard many times. The third is one the Forest Service is probably struggling with, so perhaps its employees, as well as congressmen, will be interested in your, the hikers', views.

The first basic economic fact is that to gain a day's pleasure a hiker covers 4 to 12 miles, a horse rider 15 to 25 miles, and a motorcyclist 20 to 50, even 80 miles if the trail is smooth enough. The second basic fact is that for a trail to serve motorcycles, it must be expensively reconstructed.

The Forest Service has three categories of trails. The construction and maintenance cost varies with the category, the terrain, and the amount of brush to be removed. The following are average costs from information provided by the Forest Service. Not yet included are overhead and travel expenses, which may double the maintenance cost.

Class 1 Primitive—may be a boot-beaten path for climbers or fishermen. Maintained once every three years to protect resource, not for benefit of user.

Construction cost—$0 to $2000 per mile[3]
Maintenance cost—$23.33 per mile ($70 once every 3 years)[3]

Class 2 Minimal—primarily used by hikers but can be multiple-use trails that are seldom used by horses or ORVs.

Construction cost—$2000 to $6000 per mile[3]
Maintenance cost—$100 per mile[3]

Class 3 Maximum—multiple-use trails for hikers, horses, and ORVs. They also can be heavily used hikers-only trails, such as Snow Lake and Lake Annette.

Construction cost—$4000 to $12,000 per mile[4]
Maintenance cost—$142 per mile, $170 in wilderness[3]

The costs of building motorcycle trails are suggested by the following items in the Forest Service's 1985 trail budget:[5] $59,258 for 9.2 miles of trail on Manastash Ridge, $185,107 for 16 miles of the McDonald Ridge Trail, and $87,776 for 9 miles of the Klone Peak–North Tommy Trail.

Determining the cost per person per day of trail recreation is somewhat complicated—at least enough so that the Forest Service has not made an official calculation. However, Forest Service records let me make some interesting comparisons. Two hikers-only trails near Snoqualmie Pass can be contrasted to a multiple-use trail near Twisp.

The first is a 3½-mile hikers-only trail to Lake Annette, a lovely mountain lake surrounded by forest and used by 6800 hikers in 1984.[3] Both the trail and lakeshore can withstand the pounding of 13,600 shoes. The second is a 4-mile hikers-only trail to Snow Lake used by 10,900 hikers in 1984.[3] The lake is surrounded by dramatic rock walls and fragile meadows. The fragile nature of the area, combined with heavy use, has created extensive rehabilitation problems and the need for extensive trail reconstruction. The third is 7½-mile Foggy Dew, a multiple-use trail used by about 1000 people a year.[6] The round trip of 15 miles is an excellent two-day hike, a modest one-day horse ride, and a two-hour ride for a motorcyclist. The trail was in excellent condition for hikers and an occasional horse. However, motorcycles were damaging the trails, so it was reconstructed. The better trail has increased motor use, and hikers are beginning to avoid the area—it is becoming a horse-motorcycle trail.

In the following chart, construction and rehabilitation costs are averaged over a ten-year period. Any work or cost after ten years is not counted.

	Lake Annette	Snow Lake	Foggy Dew before ORVs	Foggy Dew with ORVs
Construction cost	none	$5600*	none	$5250
Maintenance cost	$697**	$568	$750	$1069
Wilderness ranger	none	$2400	none	none
Total annual cost	$697	$8568	$750	$6319
Divided by number of users per year	6800	10,900	1000[6]	800[7]
Cost to Forest Service for a day's recreation	$0.10	$0.79	$0.75	$7.88***

* includes rehabilitation of meadows
** includes $200 litter cleanup
*** only two hours recreation for motorcyclist

If improved to accommodate motorcycle use, most existing trails must be reconstructed, at a cost of $140,000 to $560,000[4] for the 20 to 80 miles a motorcyclist needs for a day's recreation, plus maintenance, of $2840 to $11,000 a year.[3] At these figures, a short 30 miles of trail used by 1000 motorcyclists a year costs the Forest Service $25.26 for each person's day of recreation.

Most Forest Service trails were built for occasional horse use by forest patrols and were not constructed to withstand today's heavy recreational horse use. Therefore, providing 25 miles of reconstructed trail for 1000 horse riders a year costs the Forest Service $21.05[4] per rider for a day's recreation.

Most existing trails are already ideally suited for hikers, so even with heavier use the reconstruction cost is minimal; as a result, a day's recreation for a hiker on any trail used by at least 1000 hikers a year is only $0.10 to $0.79 a day.[3]

Cost to the Forest Service to provide a day's recreation on trails used by 1000 people a year is as follows:

Hikers	**Horse riders**	**Motorcycles**
$0.10 to $0.79 a day	$15 to $21 a day	$21 to $35 a day

To be sure, this simple formula cannot be applied to all trails, such as remote ones used by only a handful of hikers each year. Building new trails to be used by so few people would not be cost-effective, but minimal maintenance on those trails now existing is as important to recreationists as maintaining the Snow Lake Trail is to the thousands of hikers that use that trail.

When the economics of trails so strongly favors hikers, one wonders why the Forest Service spends so much of its limited recreation money on horses and, worse yet, on building better trails to encourage more ORV use, thereby sending hikers into national parks and fragile wilderness areas to escape machines. Many of these sanctuaries are already so full of people fleeing from machines that a person needs a permit to enter.

In the European Alps even trails used by farmers and foresters are closed to recreational use by motors. Even in Japan, where most of the machines come from, they are kept on a much tighter leash. But in America. . . .

But, only in America do letters to public officials accomplish so much.

In the state of Washington, there are approximately 350,000 self-propelled hikers and approximately 15,000 motorized trail users. With so overwhelming a ratio of 20 hikers to 1 motor, why do hikers have any problem? The answer is simple. While hikers were busy working on wilderness preservation, the ORV people and their organizations were busy lobbying legislators and working with the Forest Service to encourage more ORV facilities. The passage of the 1984 Washington Wilderness Act was wonderful, but only an additional 14 percent of the Forest Service trails were preserved. While the most spectacular rock and ice scenery in the state is now safeguarded in national parks and wilderness, by the very nature of the terrain these areas are not conducive to an extensive trail system, leaving the majority of trails used by hikers in unprotected areas. To keep the trails free of roads and motorcycles, hikers must become involved, just as the ORV people are, in both legislative and Forest Service policy making.

As an example of how warped an administrator's view of reality can be by a supposed "fairness," many trails on the east slopes of the Cascades that are closed to wheels in their upper reaches, are open to them for some distance from the trailhead. What this means is that senior citizens and families with small children, who can only manage four miles a day, must do their walking on motorized roads.

Point out to your congressman and senators the number of hikers compared to the number of motorcyclists on our trails, tell how many miles of trail a motorcyclist needs compared to a hiker's needs, given the government's cost to support the different forms of recreation, and send a copy of each letter to the regional forester. Get involved with the district rangers in your favorite hiking areas, attend forest planning meetings, and express your views on motorfree recreation.

The motorcycle people have a very effective industry-subsidized lobby, while in the past, hikers have had none. Fortunately this has now changed.[8,9] Hikers must support the new hiking organizations, hikers must speak for themselves, must take up their pens—their pencils—their typewriters—their word processors—their telephones. With whatever tool, hikers must speak! Voice (or better yet write) your opinions on how trails should be used to your congressman, senators, and the regional forester.[10]

Ira Spring

1. Clawson, Marion and Carlton S. Van Doren, Statistics on Outdoor Recreation. Washington, D.C.: Resources for the Future, Inc., 1984, page 196.
2. Washington State Interagency for Outdoor Recreation report, "ORV Dollars and You," 1985.
3. Forest Service figures from North Bend Ranger District.
4. Forest Service figures from North Bend Ranger District and Wenatchee National Forest's request for ORV funds, September 1984.
5. Wenatchee National Forest request for ORV funds, September 1984.
6. I estimated 400 hikers for two days and 200 for one day.
7. I estimated 400 motorcyclists and 200 horse riders.
8. American Hiking Society, 1701 18th Street N.W., Washington, D.C. 20009.
9. Washington Trails Association, 16812 36th West, Lynnwood, WA 98037.
10. Regional Forester, Region 6, USFS, 319 S.W. Pine Street, P.O. Box 3623, Portland, OR 97208.

INTRODUCTION

The country sampled by these 100 hikes has many characteristics in common throughout, and in common, too, with companion volumes on the region north of Stevens Pass, *100 Hikes in the North Cascades*, and the region south of Snoqualmie Pass, *100 Hikes in the South Cascades and Olympics*, as well as the volume devoted entirely to The Mountain, *50 Hikes in Mount Rainier National Park*. There are, however, significant differences from place to place caused by variations in climate, geology, elevation, and the amount and sort of human use.

The key difference may be simply expressed as *west* (maritime greenery of Puget Sound lowlands) and *east* (golden hills above the semi-arid Columbia River valley). On the windward slopes of the Cascades the precipitation is heavy enough to nourish (nearly) rain forests. The leeward slopes, in the rainshadow, often are sunny when the crest is lost in mists and drizzles, and the forests are generally more open. However, the Cascade Range is much narrower at this latitude than farther north and the contrasts in climate from one edge to the other are less marked. The hiking season is everywhere about the same because though snows pile deeper on the west, elevations average higher on the east. Past glaciation has left in all parts a legacy of sharp-sculptured peaks, plus cirque basins and scoured valleys now filled by lakes high and low—some 600 in all.

The Alpine Lakes country offers an infinity of trail experiences—short and easy hikes that can be done by small children and elders with no training or equipment for mountain travel, and long hikes, and difficult hikes, and long-and-difficult off-trail hikes which should be attempted only by the hardiest of wilderness roamers.

The hiking season in low-elevation valleys is virtually the whole year; higher, the flowers may not poke through snowbanks until late July, a mere several weeks before their frozen seeds are blanketed by the new winter's white; higher still there are no flowers ever, and no real hiking season, either, only a climbing season. There are places on the east slopes where on any day of the year a person has an excellent chance of a sunburn, and others, on the west slope, where on any day of the year a person has a good chance of getting soaking wet right through his rainproof parka, and others, on the Cascade Crest, where hikers within a mile of each other are at one and the same time gasping from thirst (east) and sputtering like a whale (west).

Administration

The Alpine Lakes area is administered by the U.S. Forest Service in the Mt. Baker-Snoqualmie and Wenatchee National Forests. A large portion of the region is in the Alpine Lakes Wilderness, where "the earth and its community of life are untrammeled by man, where man himself is a visitor who does not remain." Motorized travel (and mechanized travel, including "mountain bikes") is forbidden absolutely and horse travel is carefully regulated or at some points even eliminated; foot travel and camping are receiving increasing regulatory attention to eliminate or minimize the human impact.

Maps

Each hike description in this book lists the appropriate topographic maps (if such are available) published by the U.S. Geological Survey. These can be purchased at mountain equipment shops or map stores or by writing the U.S. Geological Survey, Federal Center, Denver, Colorado 80225. The USGS maps are the hiker's best friend.

The National Forests publish recreation maps which are quite accurate and up-to-date. These may be obtained for a small fee at ranger stations or by writing the Forest Supervisors at:

Mt. Baker-Snoqualmie National Forest
1022 1st Avenue
Seattle, WA 98104

Wenatchee National Forest
P.O. Box 811
Wenatchee, WA 98801

In the National Forests a traveler not only must have a map published by the Forest Service but it must be a *current* map; the problem—and it is a distinct pain in the lower back—is that the Forest Service is engaged in renumbering roads, made necessary when the number of roads grew so large as to require the use of more than three digits. For instance, road No. 130 became road No. 1200830, and is perhaps shown as such on the new map, though the roadside sign may be simply "830." One ranger district is using parentheses, as 1200(830), another dashes, as 1200-830, and another commas, as 1200,830.

A traveller *must* know the right numbers because in many areas the Forest Service puts no names on signs, just numbers—the new ones. Your map, if it has the old numbers, will merely deepen your confusion.—And we hate to mention it, but many of the old signs remain, with the old numbers, so that even your *new* map compounds the difficulty. A word to the wise: never leave civilization without a full tank of gas, survival rations, and instructions to family or friends on when to call out the Logging Road Search and Rescue Team.

Clothing and Equipment

Many trails described in this book can be walked easily and safely, at least along the lower portions, by any person capable of getting out of a car and onto his feet, and without any special equipment whatever.

To such people we can only say, "welcome to walking—but beware!" Northwest mountain weather, especially on the ocean side of the ranges, is notoriously undependable. Cloudless morning skies can be followed by afternoon deluges of rain or fierce squalls of snow. Even without a storm a person can get mighty chilly on high ridges when—as often happens—a cold wind blows under a bright sun and pure blue sky.

No one should set out on a Cascade or Olympic trail, unless for a brief stroll, lacking warm long pants, wool (or the equivalent) shirt or sweater, and a windproof and rain-repellent parka, coat, or poncho. (All these in the rucksack, if not on the body during the hot hours.) And on the feet—sturdy shoes or boots plus two pair of wool socks and an extra pair in the rucksack.

As for that rucksack, it should also contain the Ten Essentials, found to be so by generations of members of The Mountaineers, often from sad experience:

1. Extra clothing—more than needed in good weather.
2. Extra food—enough so something is left over at the end of the trip.
3. Sunglasses—necessary for most alpine travel and indispensable on snow.
4. Knife—for first aid and emergency firebuilding (making kindling).
5. Firestarter—a candle or chemical fuel for starting a fire with wet wood.
6. First aid kit.
7. Matches—in a waterproof container.
8. Flashlight—with extra bulb and batteries.
9. Map—be sure it's the right one for the trip.
10. Compass—be sure to know the declination, east or west.

Camping and Fires

Indiscriminate camping blights alpine meadows. A single small party may trample grass, flowers, and heather so badly they don't recover from the shock for several years. If the same spot is used several or more times a summer, year after year, the greenery vanishes, replaced by bare dirt. The respectful traveler always aims to camp in the woods, or in rocky morainal areas. These alternatives lacking, it is better to use a meadow site already bare—in technical terminology, "hardened"—rather than extend the destruction into virginal places nearby.

Particularly to be avoided are camps on soft meadows (hard rock or bare-dirt sites may be quite all right) on the banks of streams and lakes. Delightful and scenic as such sites are, their use may endanger the water purity, as well as the health of delicate plants. Moreover, a camp on a viewpoint makes the beauty unavailable to other hikers who simply want to come and look, or eat lunch, and then go camp in the woods.

Carry a collapsible water container to minimize the trips to the water supply that beat down a path. (As a bonus, the container lets you camp high on a dry ridge, where the solitude and the views are.)

Carry a lightweight pair of camp shoes, less destructive to plants and soils than trail boots.

As the age of laissez faire camping yields to the era of thoughtful management, different policies are being adopted in different places. For example, high-use spots may be designated "Day Use Only," forbidding camps. In others there is a blanket rule against camps within 100 feet of the water. However, in certain areas the rangers have inventoried existing camps, found 95 percent are within 100 feet of the water, and decided it is better to keep existing sites, where the vegetation long since has been gone, than to establish new "barrens" elsewhere. The rule in such places is "use established sites"; wilderness rangers on their rounds disestablish those sites judged unacceptable.

Few shelter cabins remain—most shown on maps aren't there anymore—so always carry a tent or tarp. *Never* ditch the sleeping area unless and until essential to avoid being flooded out—and afterward be sure to fill the ditches, carefully replacing any sod that may have been dug up.

Always carry a sleeping pad of some sort to keep your bag dry and your bones comfortable. *Do not* revert to the ancient bough bed of the frontier past.

The wood fire also is nearly obsolete in the high country. At best, dry firewood is hard to find at popular camps. What's left, the picturesque silver snags and logs, is part of the scenery, too valuable to be wasted cooking a pot of soup. It should be (but isn't quite, what with the survival of little hatchets and little folks who love to wield them) needless to say that green, living wood must never be cut; it doesn't burn anyway.

Both for reasons of convenience and conservation, the highland hiker should carry a lightweight stove for cooking (or not cook—though the food is cold, the inner man is hot) and depend on clothing and shelter (and sunset strolls) for evening warmth. The pleasures of a roaring blaze on a cold mountain night are indisputable, but a single party on a single night may use up ingredients of the scenery that were long decades in growing, dying, and silvering.

At remote backcountry camps, and in forests, fires perhaps may still be built with a clear conscience. Again, one should minimize impact by using only established fire pits and using only dead and down wood. When finished, be certain the fire is absolutely out—drown the coals and stir them with a stick and then drown the ashes until the smoking and steaming have stopped completely and a finger stuck in the slurry feels no heat. Embers can smoulder underground in dry duff for days, spreading gradually and burning out a wide pit—or kindling trees and starting a forest fire.

If you decide to build a fire, *do not make a new fire ring*—use an existing one. In popular areas patroled by rangers, its existence means this is an approved, "established" or "designated" campsite. If a fire ring has been heaped over with rocks, it means the site has been dis-established.

Litter and Garbage and Sanitation

ȮUurs is a wasteful, throwaway civilization—and something is going to have to be done about that soon. Meanwhile, it is bad wildland manners to leave litter for others to worry about. The rule among considerate hikers is: *If you can carry it in full, you can carry it out empty.*

Thanks to a steady improvement in manners over recent decades, and the posting of wilderness rangers who glory in the name of garbage-collectors, American trails are cleaner than they have been since Columbus landed. Every hiker should learn to be a happy collector.

On a day hike, take back to the road (and garbage can) every last orange peel and gum wrapper.

On an overnight or longer hike, burn all paper (if a fire is built) but

Melakwa Lake

carry back all unburnables, including cans, metal foil, plastic, glass, and papers that won't burn.

Don't bury garbage. If fresh, animals will dig it up and scatter the remnants. Burning before burying is no answer either. Tin cans take as long as 40 years to disintegrate completely; aluminum and glass last for centuries. Further, digging pits to bury junk disturbs the ground cover, and iron eventually leaches from buried cans and "rusts" springs and creeks.

Don't leave leftover food for the next travelers; they will have their own supplies and won't be tempted by "gifts" spoiled by time or chewed by animals.

Especially don't cache plastic tarps. Weathering quickly ruins the fabric, little creatures nibble, and the result is a useless, miserable mess.

Keep the water pure. Don't wash dishes in streams or lakes, loosing food particles and detergent. Haul buckets of water off to the woods or rocks, and wash and rinse there. Eliminate body wastes in places well removed from watercourses; first dig a shallow hole in the "biological disposer layer," then touch a match to the toilet paper (or better, use leaves), and finally cover the evidence. So managed, the wastes are consumed in a matter of days. Where privies are provided, use them.

Party Size

One management technique used to minimize impact in popular areas is to limit the number of people in any one group to a dozen or fewer. Hikers with very large families (or outing groups from clubs or wherever) should check the rules when planning a trip.

Pets

The handwriting is on the wall for dog owners. Pets always have been forbidden on national park trails and now some parts of wildernesses are being closed. How fast the ban spreads will depend on the owners' sensitivity, training, acceptance of responsibility, and courtesy—and on the expressed wishes of non-owners.

Where pets are permitted, even a well-behaved dog can ruin someone else's trip. Some dogs noisily defend an ill-defined territory for their master, "guard" him on the trail, snitch enemy bacon, and are quite likely to defecate on the flat bit of ground the next hiker will want to sleep on.

For a long time to come there will be plenty of "empty" country for those who hunt upland game with dogs or who simply can't enjoy a family outing without ol' Rover. However, the family that wants to go where the crowds are must leave its best friend home.

Do not depend on friendly tolerance of wilderness neighbors. Some people are so harassed at home by loose dogs that a hound in the wilderness has the same effect on them as a motorcycle. They may holler at you and turn you in to the ranger.

Dogs belong to the same family as coyotes, and even if no wildlife is visible, a dog's presence is sensed by the small wild things into whose home it is intruding.

Horses

As backcountry population grows the trend is toward designating certain trails and camps "Hiker Only," because some ecosystems cannot withstand the impact of large animals and some trails are not safe for them. However, many wilderness trails will continue to be "Hiker and Horse" (no motorcycles, no "mountain bikes") and the two must learn to get along.

Most horse riders do their best to be good neighbors on the trail and know how to go about it. The typical hiker, though, is ignorant of the difficulties inherent in maneuvering a huge mass of flesh (containing a very small brain) along narrow paths on steep mountains.

The first rule is, the horse has the right of way. For his own safety as well as that of the rider, the hiker must get off the trail—on the downhill side, preferably, giving the clumsy animal and its perilously-perched rider the inside of the tread. If necessary—as, say, on the Goat Rocks Crest—retreat some distance to a safe passing point.

The second rule is, when you see the horse approaching, do not keep silent or stand still in a mistaken attempt to avoid frightening the beast. Continue normal motions and speak to it, so the creature will recognize you as just another human and not think you a silent and doubtless dangerous monster.

Finally, if you have a dog along, get a tight grip on its throat to stop the nipping and yapping, which may endanger the rider and, in the case of a surly horse, the dog as well.

Theft

A quarter-century ago theft from a car left at the trailhead was rare. Not now. Equipment has become so fancy and expensive, so much worth stealing, and hikers so numerous, their throngs creating large assemblages of valuables, that theft is a growing problem. Not even wilderness camps are entirely safe; a single raider hitting an unguarded camp may easily carry off several sleeping bags, a couple tents and assorted stoves, down booties, and freeze-dried strawberries—maybe $1000 worth of gear in one load! However, the professionals who do most of the stealing mainly concentrate on cars. Authorities are concerned but can't post guards at every trailhead.

Rangers have the following recommendations.

First and foremost, don't make crime profitable for the pros. If they break into a hundred cars and get nothing but moldy boots and tattered T shirts they'll give up. The best bet is to arrive in a beat-up 1960 car with doors and windows that don't close and leave in it nothing of value. If you insist on driving a nice new car, at least don't have mag wheels, tape deck, and radio, and keep it empty of gear. Don't think locks help—pros can open your car door and trunk as fast with a picklock as you can with your key. Don't imagine you can hide anything from them—they know all the hiding spots. If the hike is part of an extended car trip, arrange to store your extra equipment at a nearby motel.

Be suspicious of anyone waiting at a trailhead. One of the tricks of the trade is to sit there with a pack as if waiting for a ride, watching new arrivals unpack—and hide their valuables—and maybe even striking up a conversation to determine how long the marks will be away.

The ultimate solution, of course, is for hikers to become as poor as they were in the olden days. No criminal would consider trailheads profitable if the loot consisted solely of shabby khaki war surplus.

Safety Considerations

The reason the Ten Essentials are advised is that hiking in the backcountry entails unavoidable risk that every hiker assumes and must be aware of and respect. The fact that a trail is described in this book is not a representation that it will be safe for you. Trails vary greatly in difficulty and in the degree of conditioning and agility one needs to enjoy them safely. On some hikes routes may have changed or conditions may have deteriorated since the descriptions were written. Also, trail conditions can change even from day to day, owing to weather and other factors. A trail that is safe on a dry day or for a highly conditioned, agile, properly equipped hiker may be completely unsafe for someone else or unsafe under adverse weather conditions.

You can minimize your risks on the trail by being knowledgeable, prepared and alert. There is not space in this book for a general treatise on safety in the mountains, but there are a number of good books and public courses on the subject and you should take advantage of them to increase your knowledge. Just as important, you should always be aware of your own limitations and of conditions existing when and where you are hiking. If conditions are dangerous, or if you are not prepared to deal with them safely, choose a different hike! It's better to have a wasted drive than to be the subject of a mountain rescue.

These warnings are not intended to scare you off the trails. Hundreds of thousands of people have safe and enjoyable hikes every year. However, one element of the beauty, freedom and excitement of the wilderness is the presence of risks that do not confront us at home. When you hike you assume those risks. They can be met safely, but only if you exercise your own independent judgement and common sense.

Protect This Land, Your Land

The Cascade country is large and rugged and wild—but it is also, and particularly in the scenic climaxes favored by hikers, a fragile country. If man is to blend into the ecosystem, rather than dominate and destroy, he must walk lightly, respectfully, always striving to make his passage through the wilderness invisible.

The public servants entrusted with administration of the region have a complex and difficult job and they desperately need the cooperation of every wildland traveler. Here, the authors would like to express appreciation to these dedicated men for their advice on what trips to include in this book and for their detailed review of the text and maps. Thanks are due the Supervisors of the Mt. Baker-Snoqualmie and Wenatchee National Forests, and their district rangers and other staff members.

On behalf of the U.S. Forest Service and National Park Service and The Mountaineers, we invite Americans—and all citizens of Earth—to come and see and live in their Washington Cascades, and while enjoying some of the world's finest wildlands, to vow henceforth to share in the task of preserving the trails and ridges, lakes and rivers, forests and flower gardens for future generations, our children and grandchildren, who will need the wilderness experience at least as much as we do, and probably more.

Water

Hikers traditionally have drunk the water in wilderness in confidence, doing their utmost to avoid contaminating it so the next person also can safely drink. But there is no assurance your predecessor has been so careful. No open water ever, nowadays, can be considered certainly safe for human consumption. Any reference in this book to "drinking water" is not a guarantee. It is entirely up to the individual to judge the situation and decide whether to take a chance.

In the late 1970s began a great epidemic of giardiasis, caused by a vicious little parasite that spends part of its life cycle swimming free in water, part in the intestinal tract of beavers and other wildlife, dogs, and people. Actually, the "epidemic" was solely in the press; *Giardia* were first identified in the 18th century and are present in the public water system of many cities of the world and many towns in America—including some in the foothills of the Cascades. Long before the "outbreak" of "beaver fever" there was the well-known malady, the "Boy Scout trots." This is not to make light of the disease; though most humans feel no ill effects (but become carriers), others have serious symptoms which include devastating diarrhea, and the treatment is nearly as unpleasant. The reason giardiasis has become "epidemic" is that there are more people in the backcountry—more people drinking water contaminated by animals—more people contaminating the water.

Whenever in doubt, boil the water 10 minutes. Keep in mind that *Giardia* can survive in water at or near freezing for weeks or months—a snow pond is not necessarily safe. Boiling is 100 percent effective against not only *Giardia* but the myriad other filthy little blighters that may upset your digestion or—as with some forms of hepatitis—destroy your liver.

If you cannot boil, use one of the several *iodine* treatments (chlorine compounds have been found untrustworthy in wildland circumstances), such as Potable Aqua or the more complicated method that employs iodine crystals. Rumor to the contrary, iodine treatments pose no threat to the health.

Be very wary of the filters sold in backpacking shops. One or two have been tested and found reliable (not against hepatitis) and new products are coming on the market but most filters presently available are useless or next to it.

Mount Index

LAKE SERENE

USGS Index

We are honoring the request of Forest Service personnel that we not give directions on how to find the old trail to Lake Serene, which the Forest Service now considers dangerous. In 1986 or some year soon following, the Forest Service will construct a new trail.

2 DOROTHY, BEAR, DEER, AND SNOQUALMIE LAKES

Round trip to Lake Dorothy from
  Miller River road 3 miles
Hiking time 2 hours
High point 3058 feet
Elevation gain 858 feet
Hikable June through
  mid-October
One day or backpack
USGS Skykomish, Grotto,
  Snoqualmie Lake

Round trip to Snoqualmie Lake
  from Taylor River road 14½
  miles
Hiking time 8 hours
High point 3147 feet
Elevation gain 2000 feet
USGS Snoqualmie Lake

Lying in a string on both sides of the Snoqualmie-Skykomish divide, these four large subalpine lakes once were so remote that only the sturdiest Scouts and fishermen could visit on a weekend; the usual trip was a week. Then logging roads pushed so far up the valleys that Dorothy was a mere 1½ miles from the car and Snoqualmie 2¼ miles—and there even were plans for a "Lake Dorothy Highway" that would have skirted all the shores! But as the wilderness concept gained strength a new attitude developed toward roads, not every one of which was considered permanently sacred. Logging roads were permitted to dwindle to footroads, transitional to trails, making the four lakes much lonesomer. However, renewed timber sales reopened the road on the Miller River side, so Lake Dorothy is once again the hangout of weekend rowdies with their beer busts, and the same fate may await the Taylor River road and Snoqualmie Lake. For now, though, the latter is decently remote and considerable solitude is possible for campers at the two middle lakes, Bear and Deer.

Drive US 2 east 17.5 miles from Gold Bar and just before the highway tunnel turn right, at a sign for Money Creek Campground, on Old Cascade Highway. At a Y in 1.2 miles turn right onto gravel Miller River road and drive 8.3 miles to the trailhead, 2200 feet.

The trail climbs through forest to Lake Dorothy at 1½ miles, 3058 feet.

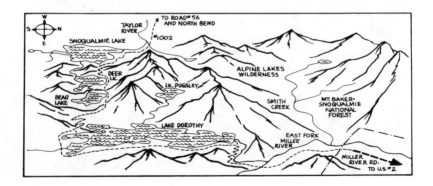

Lake Dorothy from Deer Lake trail

It follows the east side of the 2-mile-long lake, crosses the marshy inlet, begins climbing, and at 4½ miles from the road tops the 3800-foot ridge dividing the Miller and Taylor Rivers. Views are down to island-dotted Dorothy amid forest and gray-white cliffs and southeast to the dominant peak of the area, 6670-foot Big Snow Mountain.

From the pass the way is downhill to Bear Lake, 3610 feet, and, at 6 miles, Deer Lake, 3583 feet. At 6½ miles is Snoqualmie Lake, 3147 feet, second-largest of the group. The trail continues 2¼ miles down the Taylor River to the end of a closed-off logging road become pleasant foot-road, elevation 1865 feet. Amble on down a scant 6 miles, pausing to admire a series of spectacular granite-slab waterfalls, to the parking area at 1225 feet.

To drive to this point, follow the Middle Fork Snoqualmie road (Hike 91) to the Taylor River bridge and turn left 1 mile to where the Quartz Creek road goes left and the old Taylor road is barricaded.

To protect the vegetation, campers are asked to use sites 100 feet from lakeshores.

Miller River road	Old:	2522
	New:	6412
Middle Fork Snoqualmie road	Old:	2445
	New:	56

Foss River peaks from Tonga Ridge

SKYKOMISH RIVER
Alpine Lakes Wilderness

3 TONGA RIDGE– MOUNT SAWYER

Round trip to pass 6½ miles
Hiking time 3 hours
High point 4800 feet
Elevation gain 400 feet

Hikable July through October
One day or backpack
USGS Scenic

The easiest ridge walk on the west side of the Cascades, with grand views, beautiful meadows, and flowers throughout the summer.

Drive US 2 east from Skykomish 1.8 miles and turn right on Foss River road No. 68. At 1.2 miles keep right on the main road. At 2.5 miles go straight ahead at the intersection just after passing under a railroad bridge. At 3.6 miles turn left on Tonga Ridge road 7 miles. Turn right at a junction on road No. (6830)310 and continue 1.5 miles to the road-end, elevation 4400 feet.

The hike begins on an old fire trail climbing to the ridge crest. In a couple hundred feet the foot trail turns off the fire trail into forest, winds through woods a while, and then follows the ridge top in meadows. At about 1½ miles the trail leaves the crest to contour around Mt. Sawyer, finally dropping a bit to Sawyer Pass, 3 miles, 4800 feet, dividing the drainages of Burn Creek and Fisher Creek. Good campsites, and also the first water of the trip, in the gentle swale of the pass, a large green meadow (commonly called N. P. Camp) that turns a brilliant red in fall.

For a wide-view sidetrip, scramble up 5501-foot Mt. Sawyer, the second large hill seen from the Tonga River approach. Leave the trail wherever the slopes look appealing and plow upward in huckleberry brush, gaining 700 feet. Try it in late August and eat your way through delicious berries. The summit panorama includes Mt. Rainier, Mt. Baker, and Glacier Peak, plus Hinman, Daniel, Sloan, and more. Immediately below are two lakes of the Jewel Lake string, easily reached from Sawyer Pass by consulting a contour map.

The most obvious tread at Sawyer Pass is on the west side, but this is a fishermen's path toward Fisher Lake (Hike 4) and soon fades out. The main trail stays to the east side of the pass, then descends 1600 feet into valley forest, crossing several small creeks. At 5½ miles skirt a clearcut, cross another clearcut and road, and at 6 miles reach Deception Creek trail.

If pickup transportation can be arranged, interesting one-way hikes can be made from here, exiting via Deception Creek (Hike 8) or Deception Lakes and Surprise Creek (Hike 9) or Deception Pass, a sidetrip to Marmot Lake, and Hyas Lake (Hike 76).

Note: In the years before establishment of the Alpine Lakes Wilderness, its advocates bitterly protested the advance of timber sales over the ridge into the valley of Deception Creek. Though the Forest Service refused to cancel the clearcuts, under continuing pressure it is now conceding that the backdoor entrance to Tonga Ridge from road No. 6830, just below Sawyer Pass, is a gross intrusion on what was wanted as wilderness, and is allowing the road to degenerate. Presently the last 3 miles are negotiable only by truck and eventually (why not immediately?) will be closed to all wheels.

Foss River road	Old:	2622	Old:	2605A
	New:	68	New:	(6830)310
Tonga Ridge road	Old:	2605		
	New:	6803		

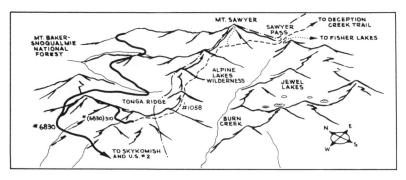

4 FISHER LAKE

Round trip to Fisher Lake 9½ miles
Hiking time 4 hours
High point 5160 feet
Elevation gain 760 feet in, 397 feet out

Hikable mid-July through mid-October
One day or backpack
USGS Scenic

Near the thronged gardens of Tonga Ridge though they are, Fisher Lake and Ptarmigan Lakes lie secluded from the mainstream of foot traffic in quiet cirques. Fishermen feet originally beat out the route, and some stretches retain their shortest-distance-to-the-fish-is-a-straight-line style.

Drive to the Tonga Ridge trailhead (Hike 3), elevation 4400 feet.

Hike 3¼ miles to Sawyer Pass, 4840 feet. At the upper end of the pass take an unmarked right about 300 feet, then go left on the unsigned Fisher Lake trail, headed south. Beyond the saddle ascend a steep hill, cross a little creek back and forth, level for a brief breather at a small marsh, and climb a second hill. While wandering with the trail through a green acre of meadow note two nameless ponds to the left.

Atop a third and final hill, 5160 feet, the trail splits. A faint path proceeds along the ridge crest to isolated June and Mary Lakes, part of the Jewel Lakes chain. Turn left and drop a final ½ mile to Fisher Lake, 4763 feet. As it curves around the east shore the main trail passes camps.

Hikers with a bit of extra time and a good bloodhound sense may continue ½ mile across the Fisher Lake outlet and along faint tread to Ptarmigan Lakes. The path meanders this way and that and several times divides. Just before a steep gully dropping to the first lake, veer right beneath cliffs to a rockslide and follow it down to the shore, 4475 feet. Nice

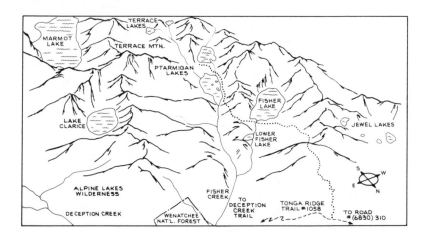

Upper Ptarmigan Lake

views up to Terrace Mountain, but no camps. Traverse south near the water on a field of boulders and at the far end find a path climbing to the second lake, 4559 feet, and a small campsite.

5 NECKLACE VALLEY

Round trip to Jade Lake 16 miles
Allow 2–3 days
High point 4600 feet
Elevation gain 3000 feet

Hikable late July through
October
USGS Skykomish, Big Snow
Mountain, Mt. Daniel

A narrow alpine valley carved from the side of Mt. Hinman and appropriately named for its string of small gems—Jade, Emerald, and Opal Lakes. Nearby are Locket and Jewel Lakes. And others. Thanks to the long trail, this is much more lonesome country than the Foss Lakes area described in Hike 6.

Drive US 2 east from Skykomish 1.8 miles. Turn right on Foss River road No. 68 for 3.6 miles to the Tonga Ridge junction, as described in Hike 3, and continue to the East Fork Foss River trail at 4.2 miles. On the left side of the road find a parking area and the trailhead, elevation 1600 feet.

The first 5 miles gain only 600 feet and are very pleasant going through forest, following the valley bottom, passing the marshes of Alturas "Lake."

The trail this far is very worthwhile in its own right and can be hiked on a day walk or a weekend backpack in May and June when the high country is buried in snow.

The trail crosses a log over the river which flows from the Hinman Glacier on Mt. Hinman and from the Lynch Glacier on Mt. Daniel. On the far bank the trail leaves the river and climbs into the hanging glacial trough, gaining 2400 feet in the 3 miles to the first gem of the necklace, Jade Lake, 4600 feet.

Necklace Valley is a delightful mixture of forest, heather, ice-polished

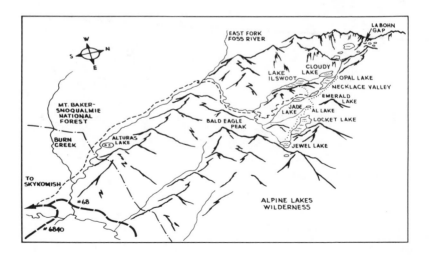

Necklace Valley, La Bohn Gap in distance

granite—and of course, the lakes. Possibilities for roaming are endless. Campsites are available along the river and at most of the lakes; the best are at Emerald.

From Emerald Lake, about ¼ mile upvalley from Jade Lake, cross a low saddle west to Jewel and Locket Lakes or cross the ridge east to Lake Ilswoot.

From the east side of Opal Lake, another ¼ mile upvalley from Emerald Lake, climb a short step up a tributary creek to Cloudy Lake.

Tougher to attain are La Bohn Lakes, set in granite bowls near the summit of 5600-foot La Bohn Gap. The off-trail route from the head of Necklace Valley goes abruptly up through cliffs, and though an easy way can be found in the vicinity of the waterfall tumbling down from the east, the "obvious" chute to the south has killed at least one hiker. No route from valley to gap can be recommended for any but experienced mountain travelers.

To preserve vegetation, campers are asked to use established sites only. Jade Lake is the most crowded; Ilswoot and Locket are quieter. Carry a stove; firewood is extremely scarce.

Foss River road   Old: 2622
                              New: 68

6

FOSS LAKES

Round trip to Copper Lake 8 miles	Hikable July through October
Hiking time 6–8 hours	One day or backpack
High point 3961 feet	USGS Big Snow Mountain
Elevation gain 2300 feet	

Lovers of alpine lakes look at the Big Snow Mountain topog map and drool. Crowded onto this single sheet are 10 large lakes and numerous small ones, the rich legacy of ancient glaciers. The West Fork Foss River trail passes four of the lakes and fishermen's paths lead to others. Don't expect privacy—the area has long been famous and extremely popular for its numerous, unusually big, and readily accessible lakes.

Drive US 2 east from Skykomish 1.8 miles. Turn right on Foss River road No. 68 for 4.2 miles to the East Fork Foss River trail, as described in Hike 5, and continue to West Fork Foss River road No. 6840 at 4.8 miles. Turn left 2 miles to the road-end and trailhead, elevation 1600 feet.

Hike an easy 1½ miles in cool forest to the first of the chain, Trout Lake, 2000 feet. Trees line the shore; through branches are glimpses of rugged cliffs above. This far makes a leisurely afternoon, and the trail is free of snow in May.

The steep, hot, 2-mile climb to Copper Lake, gaining 2000 feet, is something else in late summer. Water is plentiful but always out of reach—splashing in falls on the far hillside, rushing along a deep gully

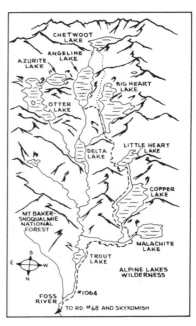

Outlet to Copper Lake

Trout Lake

below the trail. The way at last opens into the cliff-walled basin of 3961-foot Copper Lake, surrounded by alpine trees and meadows and talus slopes.

Though much can be seen in a day or weekend, 3 days or more are needed for a satisfying exploration. Copper Lake is the beginning of highland terrain, with miles of heather and blueberries amid groves of alpine trees, and glacier-smoothed rock knolls and granite buttresses. The crowds steadily diminish beyond Copper.

The lovely cirque of Malachite Lake, 4089 feet, is reached by a steep ¼-mile path branching from the main trail ½ mile before Copper Lake.

Beyond Copper Lake the main trail climbs gently along a stream, passing the best and maybe the only flower display of the trip, to 4204-foot Little Heart Lake, 1 mile from Copper, then crosses a 4700-foot ridge and drops to 4545-foot Big Heart Lake, 2½ miles from Copper; during the ridge crossing take a short sidetrip from the trail for an overlook of three lakes.

The formal trail continues beyond the outlet of Big Heart Lake 1 mile over the end of the ridge to the outlet of 4609-foot Angeline Lake. Chetwoot Lake, 4905 feet, coldest and rockiest of the group, may be reached by leaving the formal trail at about its high point on the ridge and traveling south over the very summit of the high and narrow ridge between Big Heart and Angeline Lakes, down into a saddle, and up once more over the next ridge. The route is a bit rugged but quite feasible, with a beaten footpath much of the way. From Chetwoot the upper end of Angeline Lake is readily accessible.

There are also Delta, Azurite, and Otter Lakes and a dozen or more smaller ones, many visible from the trail and each a jewel in its own right. Routes known to hardy fishermen, and even semblances of boot-beaten track, exist to all of them, but essentially these lakes are for the experienced cross-country hiker.

All camps at all the lakes are heavily used and usually crowded. Carry a stove if you want hot food or boiled drinking water. To preserve vegetation, use established sites only. At Trout Lake only several sites are designated and no others may be used; due to sanitation problems, do not fail to boil the water. Camping is very limited at Malachite, Little Heart, and Chetwoot Lakes and virtually impossible at Angeline. Copper has a large expanse of comfortable people-beaten dirt. The most scenic camping is at Big Heart.

Rock Lake

SKYKOMISH RIVER
Alpine Lakes Wilderness

7   ROCK LAKE

Round trip 4 miles
Hiking time 4 hours
High point 5640 feet
Elevation gain 1800 feet in, 1100 feet out

Hikable mid-July through September
One day or backpack
USGS Skykomish

At the south end of Maloney Ridge, hidden in folds of Malachite Peak, lies an enchanting alpine lake. However, the government never spent a nickel on the route, a fishermen's track that climbs straight up a steep rib, clambers over windfalls, edges around rock knobs—and distinctly is not for any but the most experienced and sure-footed hikers.

Drive the Foss River road (following signs to Maloney Ridge) 4.8 miles to the turnoff to West Fork Foss River road (Hike 6). Continue straight ahead on road No. 6840 to 8.1 miles and turn left on road No. 6848, passing the short trail (¼ mile) to Evans Lake and at 11.2 miles reaching the road-end, elevation 3840 feet.

The trailhead is not marked. Walk 100 feet back down the road to a culvert and turn uphill on an old cat track. In 50 feet watch left for a brushy trail that leads up to a rib. From here on the way is well-defined, skirting the top of a large clearcut. As the tread fades out, cut right into virgin forest.

The directions are now very simple: follow the rib. If the trail—always faint and often confused by fallen logs—disappears completely, return to the rib crest and continue up.

At ¾ mile is a nameless lakelet, 4630 feet, with rude campsites on the north side. Drop to the shore, bear left over the outlet, and climb the rib on the south side of the lake. The angle increases, involving hands as well as feet. At 1¼ miles is the high point, a rocky knob, 5640 feet. Skirt the knob on the left, just below the summit, and follow the rib down left to join Maloney Ridge.

At 1½ miles from the road the ridge reaches a small bench. A faint path continues onward into windfalls; the lake trail drops invisibly left, reappearing on the bench below, and thenceforth is good to Rock Lake, 4560 feet. A knoll near the outlet has campsites.

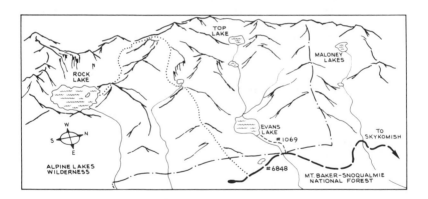

DECEPTION CREEK

Round trip to campsite 6 miles	**Hikable June through October**
Hiking time 4 hours	**One day or backpack**
High point 3200 feet	**USGS Scenic and Mt. Daniel**
Elevation gain 1400 feet	

For quick routes to lakes and views and meadows, and for easy valley-bottom strolls, go elsewhere in the Alpine Lakes Wilderness. However, for deep immersion in virgin forest and close encounters with a splendid white brawl of water, Deception Creek is the place. The trail makes an excellent exit for a loop hike, as well as a superb late-spring and early-summer walk when the high country remains monotonously wintry. Enjoy the boulders draped in licorice fern, the walls dripping delicate maidenhair fern, the bogs of wicked-looking devils club, and the blossoms of queens cup and Canadian dogwood bursting from the moss-covered forest floor.

Drive US 2 east 8 miles from Skykomish, .2 mile beyond the Deception Falls parking area, and turn right on road No. 6088, signed "Deception Creek Trail." In .4 mile pass beneath a railroad trestle to the road-end and trailhead, elevation 2000 feet.

Trail No. 1059 parallels Deception Creek a scant ½ mile, crosses at the wilderness boundary, and that's the end of easy strolling. The way gains 1000 feet to get above wooded cliffs and at 2 miles crosses a spooky log high above Sawyer Creek—the only possible crossing when the creek is in early-summer flood. From the high point, 3200 feet, at 2½ miles, the trail drops 400 feet to a delightful campsite beside Deception Creek, 2800 feet, a good turnabout.

The trail crosses the creek twice more in the next 2 miles, has numerous ups and downs, and passes several lonesome camps. At 5 miles is a junction with a trail from a nearby road on Tonga Ridge, formerly an obnoxious shortcut entry but now in process of gradual closure (Hike 3). At 7½ miles is a junction with the Deception Lakes trail; a party that enters the wilderness via Surprise Creek (Hike 9) may descend this way to exit

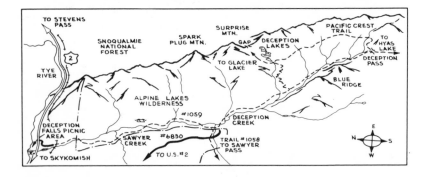

Sawyer Creek crossing

via Deception Creek, reaching the highway just 2 miles from the entry trailhead. At 10½ miles the path joins the Pacific Crest Trail at Deception Pass; any number of loops and one-way trips may be hooked into here.

Mount Daniel from Surprise Gap

SKYKOMISH RIVER
Alpine Lakes Wilderness

9 SURPRISE LAKE AND MOUNTAIN

Round trip to Surprise Lake 8½
  miles
Hiking time 5 hours
High point 4500 feet
Elevation gain 2300 feet
Hikable late June through
  October
One day or backpack
USGS Scenic

Round trip to Surprise Mountain
  15½ miles
Hiking time 9–12 hours
High point 6330 feet
Elevation gain 4100 feet
Hikable late July through
  October

Surprise Lake mirrors a ring of green trees and white granite. Glacier Lake adds the cliffs of Surprise Mountain, whose summit is the supreme grandstand for viewing the glacial brilliance of Daniel and Hinman, forest deeps of Deception Creek, and peaks from Baring to Monte Cristo to Glacier to Cashmere.

Drive US 2 east from Skykomish 10 miles. Just after the highway makes a bend left, go off right on an unsigned road that crosses the Tye River to the hamlet of Scenic, service center for the Burlington-Northern Railroad's Cascade Tunnel, whose west portal is nearby. Drive over the railroad tracks and in a hundred feet turn right on a sideroad with a hiker-trail symbol. In about ¼ mile, before the road starts a rough ascent, park, elevation 2200 feet.

Walk the road (some cars drive, but not happily) ¼ mile, following the powerline swath to the trail, which quickly leaves hot brush for cool trees. No other hike in the vicinity offers a more joyful forest, so many excellent waterfalls, and exactly the proper trickles and gushes to splash face and head (despite green shadows, these can become quite dry, particularly on switchbacks of the final mile, where the trail parallels a continuous cataract up into the hanging valley). A picnic lunch atop a granite buttress at Surprise Lake, 4508 feet, 4 miles from the trailhead, climaxes a nice day.

Having passed the old route of the Pacific Crest Trail just before Surprise Lake, on the way to Glacier Lake the valley trail passes the new route. The valley trail avoids Glacier, 4806 feet, but sidepaths give easy access. At 1½ miles from the Surprise outlet the trail passes the site of the old shelter cabin, and in a scant ½ mile more it opens out in a basin of granite blocks and green lawns and meltwater creeks and flowers a-rioting. Here at the foot of Surprise Mountain's 1000-foot walls is a junction, 5100 feet.

The new Crest Trail turns right and climbs to 5900-foot Pieper Pass, the (long) way to Deception Lakes and points south and the start of off-trail explorations to Spark Plug Mountain and Spark Plug Lake.

The old, abandoned Crest Trail climbs in a scant ½ mile of rock gardens (or snow—in early summer, be careful) to Surprise Gap, 5780 feet. This is the short way, 1¼ miles from the gap, down to 5053-foot Deception Lakes, very nice. For the views turn right at the gap and climb 1 steep mile through parkland and meadows and marmots to the summit of Surprise Mountain, 6330 feet. Naught remains of the lookout cabin except a litter of fragments—and the metal post that was the base of the firefinder. The views! Precipitously down spectacular cliffs to the lakes. Across the broad valley to the gleaming ice. West to saltwater, north to volcanoes, east to Enchantments.

Camps are numerous at and near both lakes and at the site of the old shelter cabin. Wood is scarce at most; carry a stove. To preserve vegetation, campers are asked to shun the shores. Carry water and camp near the summit of Surprise and see more stars than are dreamt of in your astronomy charts.

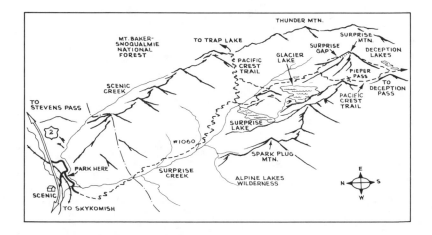

10   HOPE LAKE AND MIG LAKE

Round trip to Mig Lake 4 miles
Hiking time 3 hours
High point 4650 feet
Elevation gain 1650 feet

Hikable mid-July through
  September
One day or backpack
USGS Stevens Pass

Fields of heather and blueberries and clumps of sturdy subalpine trees ring two alpine lakes. Though small by Alpine Lakes Wilderness standards, Hope and Mig offer pleasant camping and are excellently located

Mig Lake

for exploring the Pacific Crest Trail north toward Stevens Pass and south to Trap Lake.

Drive US 12 east from Skykomish 12 miles, cross Tunnel Creek bridge, and just before the highway widens to four lanes go right on road No. 6095, extremely rough; the typical family car may be happier to park at a large open area near the highway. At .4 mile the road forks; go right on road No. (6095)110, crossing a cement bridge. At .8 mile, the next junction, stay left, avoiding a second bridge. At 1 mile the road splits again. Go left, steeply up on road No. (6095)112, then left again on road No. 6095(115), and at 1.1 miles find Tunnel Creek trailhead No. 1061, elevation 3000 feet.

Note: In 1984 the trail was rerouted due to logging and a temporary route was roughed in. This trail, starting from the end of road No. 6095(110), will be used until the new trailhead is completed.

Ascend the valley in cool green forest on tread kept in superb condition by adopt-a-trail volunteers of The Mountaineers. The way is steep and never in sight of Tunnel Creek until the final ¼ mile. At 1½ miles is Hope Lake, 4400 feet; the large campsites are definite invitations to spend time exploring.

From Hope Lake turn left on Interstate 2000 (the Pacific Crest Trail) ½ mile to Mig Lake, 4650 feet, and more camps.

These two are only the beginning of the lakes. North 2 miles from Mig Lake is Swimming Deer Lake, off on a sidetrail. Josephine and Susan Jane are a bit beyond. South from Hope 3 miles along a scenic ridge are the rockbound shores of Trap Lake.

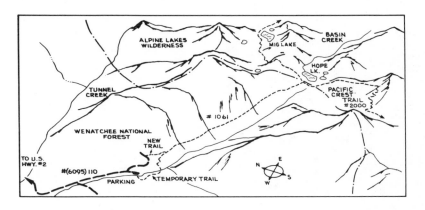

11 SWIMMING DEER LAKE

Round trip to Swimming Deer Lake 10 miles
Hiking time 8 hours
High point 5200 feet
Elevation gain 1600 feet in, 1000 feet out

Hikable mid-July through mid-October
One day or backpack
USGS Stevens Pass

A person's fondest recollections of this stretch of the Cascade Crest may well be not of hiking in sunshine but in a fog or slow-drifting clouds, when distant views do not compete with foreground miniatures of heather and blueberries and Christmas trees, and when mists hide until the last moment surprises around turns in the trail—little marshes and ponds, flower-rimmed meadow lakelets, bigger lakes in rock-walled cirques, and perhaps a swimming deer.

Drive US 2 to Stevens Pass, and just east of the Forest Service residence on the south side of the highway turn into the large parking lot, elevation 4061 feet.

Though the Pacific Crest Trail sets out up ski slopes, it is plainly and solidly built, ascending steadily in trees and rockslides to the Cascade Crest at 1½ miles, 5150 feet. Though it then descends ¼ mile to a power-line swath and service road, markers clearly delineate the route to undisturbed terrain. The trail traverses patches of forest, wet meadows rich in

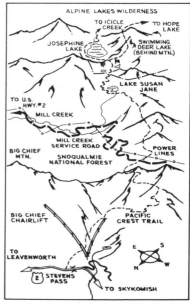

Queen's cup

Pacific Crest Trail near Lake Susan Jane

flower color, and open talus with views out Mill Creek to the Nason Creek valley and Nason Ridge. At 3½ miles is Lake Susan Jane, 4595 feet, a modest tarn tucked in a tiny cirque, cliffs above, valley below. Here are the first camps, very pleasant, if heavily pounded.

Shift down to climb through meadows by ponds to a 4950-foot saddle— the boundary of the Alpine Lakes Wilderness—and a junction at 4 miles, 5000 feet, with Icicle Creek trail No. 1551. This is the route to Chain Lakes (Hike 12) and also, immediately below, Josephine Lake, 4681 feet, large and rocky and forest-shored; campsites near the outlet.

Enjoy the views down to the blue lakes and out to the Stuart Range and continue south on the Crest Trail, climbing heather fields to round the corner of another open ridge at 5200 feet. In 1 mile from the junction find a sidetrail down to the broad parkland bench, 4890 feet, where the shores of Swimming Deer Lake wind in and out of clumps of subalpine trees, and camps on wooded knolls suggest stopping over a night or two for explorations.

If pickup transportation can be arranged, a one-way hike can be made south on the Crest Trail, exiting via Tunnel Creek (Hike 10) or Surprise Creek (Hike 9).

12 CHAIN LAKES— DOELLE LAKES

Round trip to Chain Lakes 22 miles
Allow 3–4 days
High point 5700 feet
Elevation gain 3600 feet in 1600, feet out

Hikable late July through September
USGS Stevens Pass

The most spectacular peak in this corner of the Cascades is the 6807-foot fang of Bulls Tooth, highest of a mile-long line of granite splinters and blocks. Beneath the ridge's cliffs on one side lie the two Doelle Lakes in cirques scooped from the granite, and beneath it on the other, in a mile-long glacial trough, lie the three Chain Lakes, so deeply shadowed the snow lasts late and comes early and the trees grow few and small in arctic meadowlands. If these aren't attractions enough, the spot is among the lonesomest in the Alpine Lakes Wilderness because no matter which approach is chosen the miles are many and the elevation gain much; the access described here is about as easy as the trip can be done.

Hike the Pacific Crest Trail 4 miles from Stevens Pass to a junction, 4960 feet, with Icicle Creek trail No. 1551 (Hike 11). Follow it left and down, past campsites at Josephine Lake, 4681 feet, and more near the junction with Whitepine Creek trail (Hike 13), an alternate entry route. At 3½ miles from the Crest Trail reach the junction with Chain Lakes trail No. 1569, 3800 feet. This is at a point on the Icicle Creek trail 8½ miles from the Icicle road, another and somewhat easier alternate entry (Hike 30).

The ascent of Chain Creek valley begins with a dizzying series of short switchbacks in forest, concludes with a steady sidehill climb in trees and openings that give looks out over Icicle country. At 2½ miles, 5628 feet, hard labor abruptly ceases at the lip of the hanging trough and shores of the first lake, long and narrow and rocky. As it ends the second lake begins, the valley broadening out in parkland and meadow. Cross the out-

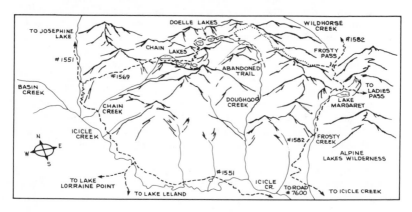

Upper Doelle Lake

let of the second lake, go left, by a string of ponds and jumbles of giant granite blocks, around the corner of a delightful knoll, and at 11 miles from Stevens Pass come to the final and most magical lake, 5690 feet, amid a broad flat of grass and flowers meandered by cold little creeks from snowfields on slopes of the crags.

The bad news is that this section of the Cascades is the stomping grounds of a few (but too many) old-timey, heavy-riding cavalry, including certain professional packers whose licenses the Forest Service darn well ought to revoke. These packers scorn no-trace camping, limber up chainsaws and double-bitted axes to log the subalpine forest, tether stock in fragile meadows and allow them to decorate the lakes, and let the bean cans and whiskey bottles fall where they may. Drastic action by the Forest Service is essential to prevent this minority of horsemen from continuing to mangle the gardens.

Nevertheless, scenic and nonbrutalized camps can be found, bases for clambering the ridges and exploring nooks. To start, from the junction at the second lake go left, then left again before the third lake on the 1-mile trail steeply up talus to a 6200-foot notch in Bulls Tooth ridge and steeply down heather gardens to Doelle Lakes, 5775 and 5635 feet, deep and cliff-walled.

Experienced wildland navigators may neatly exit—and make a loop— from Doelle Lakes by proceeding down the abandoned Doughgod Creek trail ¾ mile, passing the wide meadow-marsh basin of a filled-in lake, crossing a rocky rib, and dropping steeply to the base of a rockslide rising from the left side of the trail. At a large rock cairn leave the Doughgo trail and ascend a faint path across a brushy talus and up a wooded draw to a four-way intersection. Turn right on a meager but definite (if intermittent) track that traverses meadows and blueberries and silver snags of an old burn 2 miles to Frosty Pass. Return to square one via Frosty Creek and Icicle Creek trails.

13 WHITEPINE CREEK

Round trip to Mule Creek Camp 12
 miles
Hiking time 7 hours
High point 3600 feet
Elevation gain 800 feet

Hikable July through
 mid-October
One day or backpack
USGS Wenatchee Lake,
 Chiwaukum Mountains,
 Stevens Pass

Curious about what it was like to hike in the Cascades when your daddy was a boy? Here's a valley for getting the feel of the olden days, when trail crews came through only once in every so many years to chop the brush in avalanche swaths and saw through windfalls, when the horses of sheepherders and hunters churned every stretch of wet tread to a mudbath, and when to meet another human being was to be as startled as Robinson Crusoe was by Friday. Aside from the solitude there is quiet virgin forest. Lonesome camps are great places to sit around the fire listening to coyotes sing.

Drive US 2 east from Stevens Pass 14 miles, west from Coles Corner 6.6 miles, and turn off on Whitepine road No. 6950. Roads branch in every direction, all unmarked, many leading to clearcuts on land owned by Longview Fiber; stick with the best-maintained and most-graveled 4 miles to the end and the Whitepine trailhead, elevation 2800 feet.

Trail No. 1582 begins in an old clearcut, enters open forest, and commences a gradual ascent in sound and occasional sight of the creek, occasional cliff bands giving views over the valley.

At 1 mile enter Alpine Lakes Wilderness and at 2½ miles pass a string of camps and the junction with the Wildhorse trail (Hike 14), 3200 feet. Take the right fork and in 500 feet cross Whitepine Creek on a horse bridge. Since most traffic goes the Wildhorse way, to Frosty Pass, the Whitepine way now leaps the generation gap into the remote past. Beyond a small camp at the site of long-gone Arrowhead Guard Station the trail alternates between forest and avalanche brush to a grassy little meadow at 6 miles, 3600 feet. Here, at the base of the old Mule Creek sheep driveway, is a good turnaround for a day or weekend hike.

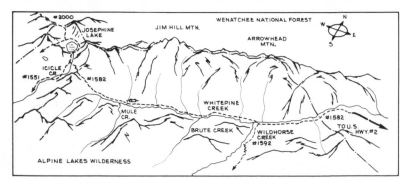

To continue is to delve deeper into the past than some hikers might like, the brush denser and the mudholes deeper. From the camp the trail crosses a wide avalanche path terminating in the boulders and gravel and mud of a blowout flood. Clamber across and enter forest for the last time, climbing to the timbered saddle, 7¾ miles, 4640 feet, between Whitepine and Icicle Creek drainage. A final ½ mile drops to the Icicle trail, 4400 feet (Hikes 13 and 30).

Whitepine Creek road   Old: 266
                       New: 6950

Small tributary of Whitepine Creek

Upper Wildhorse Creek valley

NASON CREEK
Alpine Lakes Wilderness

WILDHORSE CREEK

Round trip to Frosty Pass 18½ miles
Allow 3–4 days
High point 5700 feet
Elevation gain 2900 feet plus ups and downs

Hikable mid-July through September
USGS Wenatchee Lake and Chiwaukum Mountains

The ordinary way to route a valley trail is to stay down in deep woods near the creek, then finish with a quick climb to headwater meadowlands. The Wildhorse trail disdains the ordinary, instead begins with a quick climb to timberline, then rolls for miles in an old burn, through flowers and huckleberries and broad views on big-sky slopes of the Chiwaukum Mountains. A party may be content with scenery of the first timberline camp, continue to Frosty Pass and the Ladies Pass lake country, or explore off-trail to lofty tundras and craggy peaks.

Drive to Whitepine Creek trailhead, elevation 2800 feet, and hike 2½ miles to the junction at 3200 feet (Hike 13).

Wildhorse trail No. 1592 instantly sets about escaping the trees, at 4½ miles passing the first of many camps by streams tumbling from high basins, and at 5 miles, 5000 feet, breaking free of forest. Henceforth the way is a yo-yo traverse for miles, gaining little elevation, giving continuous views over Wildhorse and Whitepine country. The fly in the pudding is that this is the main horse route to Ladies Pass, and at least one of the professional packers who bring in fishermen and hunters is guilty of leaving behind incredible amounts of garbage. Even the clean-living horses stomp the tread to mud, requiring fancy footwork by hikers who don't like dirty socks.

Along the way the canny wildland traveler may ascend meadows on bits of old path to the stunning scenery of Deadhorse Pass, 7200 feet, stop overnight at any of several nice creek camps, or at 8¼ miles find an abandoned trail climbing 1½ miles to Grace Lakes, 6242 feet.

At 8¾ miles is the last camp before the final climb to Frosty Pass, 5700 feet, 9¼ miles, and the junction with the Icicle Ridge trail (Hike 21). To the left ¾ mile are overcrowded camps at Lake Mary, everybody's destination (Hike 36). To the right ¼ mile along the meadow saddle is Frosty Pass, from which Frosty Creek trail No. 1593 drops ¾ mile to Lake Margaret's small and over-used camps. A sign at the pass, "Horse Camps," points the short distance to Table Camp, often deserted when Lake Mary is Tent City and offering long vistas out the Wildhorse. The trail actually continues past the camp, eventually leading to Doelle Lakes (Hike 12), but only if you don't get lost.

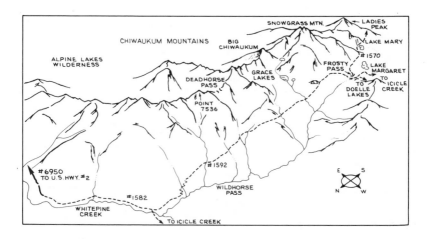

15

LAKE ETHEL

Round trip 9 miles
Hiking time 5 hours
High point 5700 feet
Elevation gain 3300 feet

Hikable mid-July through
  September
One day or backpack
USGS Wenatchee Lake

Exactly where deep forest yields to steep green meadows at the north end of the Chiwaukum Mountains, Lake Ethel perches in its cirque, on the border of the open, roaming country. Getting there, though, is less than half the fun—three times the trail crosses a private (gated) logging road and is frequently in view of clearcuts extending to the boundary of the Alpine Lakes Wilderness, which doesn't (not yet) include even the lake.

Drive US 2 east from Stevens Pass 16.3 miles to road No. 6940 on the southeast side of the highway. Cross Nason Creek and take the first left .2 mile, bumping over railroad tracks to a junction under the powerlines. Take the left, signed "Not Maintained for Passenger Cars," .2 teeth-rattling mile to a split. Stay left .2 mile to the next split; go right. The road returns to the powerlines, where most cars will request they be parked before dropping to ford a creek and rumbling over several gravel bars. In .2 mile the road returns to forest for a final peaceful .2 mile to the trailhead at the first switchback, elevation 2400 feet.

The way begins on an old road which soon narrows to well-graded trail. Views are excellent over highway, airstrip, powerlines, and train tracks to the green upsweep of Nason Ridge. In 1½ steady-climbing miles the trail attains a ridge above Gill Creek and stays there 2½ miles, in forest except where logged. Just before 2 miles is the first road crossing and shortly before 3 miles the last.

At 3½ miles, 5700 feet, the trail abruptly turns left and drops from the ridge to Gill Creek, at 4¼ miles joining the old trail that followed Gill

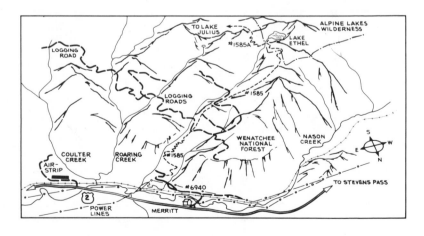

Creek until the valley was clearcut by heirs of the Northern Pacific Land Grant. Go right ¼ mile to a junction with Upper Roaring Creek trail No. 1585A, leading to Lake Julius and McCue Ridge (Hike 16). Continue straight to Lake Ethel, 5500 feet, and a large camping area.

Hikers with happy feet may follow the Upper Roaring Creek trail 1 mile to the open ridge between Gill Creek and Roaring Creek, and 1½ more miles to fine views of Lake Julius, Lake Ethel, McCue Ridge, and especially the long rampart of the high and mighty Chiwaukum Mountains.

Lake Ethel road   Old: 2734
                   New: 6940

Nason Creek valley from Lake Ethel trail

16 LAKE JULIUS AND LOCH EILEEN

Round trip to Loch Eileen from
Lake Ethel trailhead 17 miles
Round trip from Lake Ethel 9
miles
Allow 2 days
High point 6000 feet
Elevation gain 4000 feet in, 700
feet out
Hikable mid-July through
mid-September
USGS Wenatchee Lake and
Chiwaukum Mountains

Round trip to Loch Eileen from
Chiwaukum Creek trailhead 26
miles
Round trip from Chiwaukum
Lake 9½ miles
Allow 2–3 days
High point 5900 feet
Elevation gain 3400 feet in, 800
feet out

Two lovely lakes sit at the edge of some of the finest highlands of the
Alpine Lakes Wilderness. However, it seems that into every wilderness
idyll a little horror story must fall. The infamous Northern Pacific Land
Grant of 1864 put much of the surrounding region in private hands, and
in 1973, despite strenuous efforts by conservationists, Wenatchee National Forest and Pack River Lumber Company began building a system
of roads to log both private and public timber. Pack River was sold to
Longview Fiber, which intends to continue where Pack River left off.
Take the hike—and return angry.

The old Lake Julius trail followed a ridge above Roaring Creek, crossing a Pack River logging road three times, which was bad enough, but
Longview Fiber intends to run a road all the way up the ridge, crossing
the trail seven more times, leaving the Forest Service no choice but to
forget it. This leaves two other approaches—but neither of these is safe in
wilderness either, so stay angry enough to do something about saving
them.

Lake Ethel approach: Drive to Lake Ethel trailhead, elevation 2400
feet, and hike 4¼ miles to the junction, 5500 feet, just below the lake
(Hike 15).

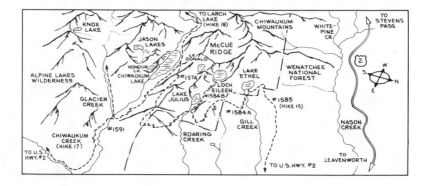

Loch Eileen

Turn left on Upper Roaring Creek trail No. 1584A, cross Gill Creek, and climb steep woods to an open saddle, 4¾ miles, 5800 feet, overlooking Roaring Creek and McCue Ridge. Wander the east side of the ridge on a broad bench, passing from lush meadows to delicate rock gardens. Tread is faint in the greenery; watch for small trail signs in the trees, and if these are lacking, scout around for a path that continues—game traces soon fade.

The way leaves the ridge, descends open slopes, switchbacks down open forest to Roaring Creek and a junction at 7 miles, 5100 feet. Take trail No. 1584B up the valley ¼ mile to Lake Julius, 5200 feet, and numerous camps. The trail rounds the north shore and climbs steeply to Loch Eileen, 5500 feet; camping here is limited.

Chiwaukum Creek approach: Though longer, the forest is magnificent, Chiwaukum Lake beautiful, and the views from McCue Ridge outstanding. A short stretch of the trail is on private land and may be messed up by loggers.

Drive to Chiwaukum Creek trailhead, elevation 2200 feet, and hike 7 miles, rounding Chiwaukum Lake, 5200 feet, to the junction with McCue Ridge trail No. 1574. (Right of way on the Chiwaukum Creek Road was in dispute in 1985. Until resolved, come prepared to hike four extra miles. See Hike 17.)

Ascend well-graded trail 1½ miles to the crest of McCue Ridge, 5750 feet and timbered; for the views walk a few hundred feet east to a big patch of snowbrush and gaze over the vast Chiwaukum valley to the Chiwaukum Mountains, culminating in the 8000-foot peaks of Snowgrass, and to the Cashmere Crags of the Stuart Range.

The trail drops 250 feet from the crest to intersect the Lake Julius trail. The right fork, to US 2, is abandoned; go left on trail No. 1591, partly on Longview Fiber land fated to be logged and thus planned to be rerouted by the Forest Service. The way descends open forest into Roaring Creek valley, crosses the creek on a sturdy bridge, and at 11¾ miles, 5600 feet, meets trail No. 1584A from Lake Ethel, leading to Lake Julius and Loch Eileen, 13 miles from the road.

For explorations, scramble from the south shore of Loch Eileen up to Lake Donald, tucked beneath McCue Ridge, or roam the 7000-foot-plus summits of the Chiwaukum Mountains, discovering tiny cirques and hidden meadows.

17 CHIWAUKUM CREEK

Round trip to Lake Flora 20 miles
Allow 3–4 days
High point 5700 feet
Elevation gain 3500 feet

Hikable mid-July through
September
USGS Chiwaukum Mountains

The most popular route to meadow highlands of the exceedingly popular "Mormon Lakes" is from the other side of the mountain (Hike 36), which means the trail population is denser there and the camps more thronged. This route is lonesomer, and the only thing the valley itself needs to be acclaimed a Cascade classic is complete protection within wilderness, which it does not now have.

Drive US 2 east 25.8 miles from Stevens Pass or west 1 mile from Tumwater Campground and turn south on Chiwaukum Creek road No. 7908. In 2 miles are the road-end and trailhead, elevation 2200 feet.

(**Note:** A subdivision into lots for private homes may bar the road to public vehicles, adding nearly 2 miles to the hike, unless the Forest Service can straighten things out. However, any "keep out" signs to the contrary, the public has guaranteed legal *foot* rights along the road.)

Trail No. 1571 ascends imperceptibly, upsy-downsy, touching the stream at small camps. The forest in the narrow, steep-walled valley is deep-shadowed and big-tree and mossy and spring-oozy, the most enchanting woods walk in the vicinity and a joyous easy-afternoon stroll. The climax of such trips, the standard turnaround point, used to be at 2½

Grindstone Mountain from Ladies Pass

miles in groves of giant ponderosa pines that sent tree huggers into delirium. They therefore fought bitterly to prevent the loggers who had climbed the other side of McCue Ridge from descending here. They lost. The groves were butchered. It is some satisfaction that their uproar caused the harvesting to be not a clearcut but "selective" (selecting all the big trees) and the access road from the ridge to be put to bed (for cars, not for motorcycles, whose racket intrudes what is otherwise a wheelfree valley). Indeed, a hiker who fails to notice the stumps will suppose the forest to be virgin, if mediocre. Those who remember the ponderosas moan and scream the whole mile of stump-lined trail.

Virgin and superb forest is reentered and at 4 miles, 3300 feet, creek and trail split. Shortly after crossing the stream on a bridge, North Fork Chiwaukum trail No. 1591 goes right to Chiwaukum Lake (Hike 18). Stay left on trail No. 1571 along the South Fork.

The deep-green slot of a valley opens out to wider and airier dimensions, forest interspersed with rockslides and avalanche brush. At 5½ miles, 3700 feet, is a pleasant, grassy camp by the junction with Painter Creek trail (Hike 20). The way climbs a valley step, passing a splendid falls where the creek tumbles over ledges of gaudy gneiss, and levels out to Timothy Meadow, 6½ miles, 4000 feet, the tall grass and bright flowers ringed by shining-white aspen trees, a favorite campsite.

At 7 miles, 4100 feet, is the overgrown junction with Index Creek trail. The valley head now can be seen, an abrupt termination in a steep-walled amphitheater from which escape seems impossible. The trail crosses the South Fork (easily, the stream now much reduced in size) at 8¾ miles and again at 9 miles and then finds the escape route, squirming up the headwall in short switchbacks and, at 10 miles, 5700 feet, suddenly flattening out in heather meadows of Lake Flora. Just across a spur in a separate cirque is the patriarch of all these lovely lady lakes, Lake Brigham.

The South Fork trail dreamily roams a final mile upward in flowers to Ladies Pass, 6800 feet, and ends. But the trip has just begun, for here is the junction with Icicle Ridge trail (Hike 21), and the sky-surrounded tundras of Snowgrass Mountain await above.

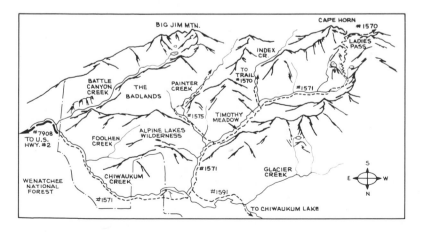

18 CHIWAUKUM LAKE– LARCH LAKE

Round trip to Larch Lake 20 miles
Allow 2–3 days
High point 6078 feet
Elevation gain 3878 feet

Hikable mid-July through
   mid-October
USGS Chiwaukum Mountains

In the shadow of the tall, rugged Chiwaukum Mountains lie two lakes rimmed by rocks and groves of larch and basecamps for high wandering. The approach is as happy as the destination—in lovely forest, by comfortable camps, with charming views of the stream, including a cascading waterfall just above one of three handsome bridges.

Drive to the end of Chiwaukum Creek road, elevation 2200 feet, and hike trail No. 1571 to the forks of creek and trail at 4 miles, 3300 feet. (Right of way on the Chiwaukum Creek Road was in dispute in 1985. Be prepared to add four extra miles to the round trip total until the matter is resolved. See Hike 17.)

Go right on North Fork Chiwaukum trail No. 1591, climbing over a large terminal moraine of the ancient valley glacier, then winding around a large marsh, descendant of the former moraine-dammed lake. At 6 miles cross Glacier Creek to a sprawling horse camp, the turnaround for hooves; beyond here the valley is hiker-only. The valley head in view, the trail steeply and hotly ascends a 1200-foot step in the old glacial trough via a gigantic talus, the excellent views of valley and Chiwaukum Mountains good excuses for pausing to gasp and pant. At 7½ miles the top of the step is attained and the way traverses ½ mile beneath rugged cliffs to Chiwaukum Lake, 8 miles, 5210 feet.

The path follows the shore, passing campsites, ½ mile to a junction with McCue Ridge trail (Hike 16), and proceeds beyond the lake to more camps in Ewing Basin, a flat ½ mile long and ¼ mile wide.

A way trail crosses the basin and a small creek and climbs steeply through forest and meadows to Larch Lake, 10 miles, 6078 feet, and

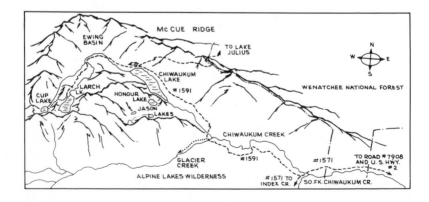

Larch Lake and Chiwaukum Mountains

many good camps. To preserve vegetation, here and elsewhere, hikers are asked to use established sites.

Explorations abound. From Chiwaukum Lake cross the outlet to Honour Lake and scramble up the hill to Jason Lakes. From Larch Lake ascend gardens to tiny Cup Lake, set at 6443 feet in a north-facing cirquelet that doesn't melt free of snow until September, if then. Find an old way trail and continue to the crest of the Chiwaukum Mountains in arctic-barren fellfields of 7200-foot Deadhorse Pass, overlooking Wildhorse and Whitepine Creeks.

Chiwaukum Creek road   Old: 265
                               New: 7908

19 LAKE AUGUSTA

Round trip to Lake Augusta 18 miles
Allow 2–3 days
High point 6854 feet
Elevation gain 4500 feet in, 350 feet out
Hikable mid-July through September
USGS Chiwaukum Mountains

Loop trip through The Badlands 23 miles
Allow 3–4 days
High point 7300 feet
Elevation gain 7000 feet
Hikable August through mid-September

A spur ridge juts 4 miles north from Icicle Ridge to The Badlands, crags and tundra on the crest, lakes filling meadow cirques scooped from the flanks, forests in deep green valleys below. Lake Augusta is the star of the waters, the meadow basin so popular that parts of the trail have been beaten to calf-deep dust by hooves and boots, other parts to knee-deep mud. Big Jim Mountain, 7763 feet, is the star of the skies, the dominant peak of the area, urgently calling lovers of these tiny alpine flowers that somehow eke out existence among its stones. Of the two approaches described here, the loop is more strenuous, less populated.

Drive US 2 to the Wenatchee River bridge opposite Tumwater Campground and turn west on Hatchery Creek road No. 7905, passing summer homes. At 1.2 and 2.2 miles stay right at unmarked forks. At 2.6 miles is

Overlooking upper Painter Creek valley drainage from a shoulder of Big Jim Mountain

a large parking area on the right side of the road, elevation 2800 feet.

Hatchery Creek approach: Hatchery Creek trail No. 1577 sets out on a stiff climb through brush, switchbacks up open forest, and at 2¼ miles crosses one of the path's rare streams; shortly beyond is a one-tent camp, 4600 feet, with fine views over the Wenatchee River valley. At 3 miles, 5300 feet, the trail splits. The Badlands trail No. 1576, return leg of the loop, goes right.

The Hatchery Creek trail continues leftward, the angle relenting to begin a rollercoaster over open ridges and colorful gardens. At 5½ miles is a secluded meadow, a nice camp. At 6½ miles, 6700 feet, Hatchery Creek trail intersects Icicle Ridge trail No. 1570. Turn right, drop to 6350 feet and camps in the meadows of Cabin Creek, and finish the climb to Lake Augusta, 9 miles, 6860 feet.

How good it is. But not enough. A hiker must not come this far without following the trail up to the 7300-foot saddle in Big Jim Ridge for long views to Mt. Rainier and close, exciting views of the Chiwaukum Mountains.

The Badlands loop: Descend from the 7300-foot saddle, the way obscure in lush meadows near timberline; head straight down and watch for cairns. At 1½ miles from Lake Augusta are little Carter Lake, 6160 feet, several small, damp camps, and the intersection with Painter Creek trail No. 1575 (Hike 20). Turn right ¼ mile down Painter Creek to a second creek crossing and several pleasant camps. The path continues along the open valley in lush meadows to the final crossing of Painter Creek, on a bridge, at 5¼ miles from Lake Augusta. Here are the last campsites of the loop.

A short bit beyond, at 5200 feet, 16 miles from the start of the hike, turn uphill on The Badlands trail, climbing steeply to a grassy ridge crest, 6200 feet, that is anything but bad. Wind on over the ridge and down to Battle Canyon Creek, 19 miles. Climb 1 mile back to Hatchery Creek trail to close the loop.

Hatchery Creek road   Old: 2528
                                    New: 7905

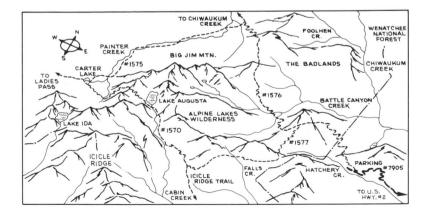

Fording the South Fork Chiwaukum Creek

NASON CREEK
Alpine Lakes Wilderness

20 INDEX CREEK– PAINTER CREEK LOOP

Loop trip 24¼ miles
Allow 3–4 days
High point 6700 feet
Elevation gain 4000 feet

Hikable August through
mid-September
USGS Chiwaukum Mountains

Peaceful valley forests, flowery alpine meadows, waterfalls and high ridges, tremendous views, and considerable solitude—who could ask for anything more? Don't complain about the absence of bridges at several crucial stream crossings—they keep out the hikers who aren't serious.

Drive to the Chiwaukum Creek road-end, elevation 2200 feet, and hike South Fork Chiwaukum Creek trail No. 1571 to an intersection at 5½ miles with Painter Creek trail, the return leg of the loop, and continue past the camps at Timothy Meadows to the takeoff of Index Creek trail at 7 miles, 4100 feet. (Come prepared to hike two extra miles each way if the Chiwaukum Creek road is gated. See Hike 17.)

Index Creek trail receives little use and less maintenance, and from a small clearing thigh-high in greenery it plunges into head-high brush.

Push through to South Fork Chiwaukum Creek and wade, ford, splash, or (in late summer) leap across.

The way climbs steadily 1 mile to a crossing of Index Creek, enters forest and trail-bog, and at about 2 miles from the Chiwaukum trail levels out in a broad beaver meadow, the dams abandoned but the ponds remaining. In the next ¾ mile the way passes several camps, leaves meadows, and recrosses the creek. At 2¾ miles from South Fork Chiwaukum Creek (9¾ miles from the road-end) is the intersection with Icicle Ridge trail No. 1570, elevation 4800 feet.

Turn left and climb from the dense pine forest to subalpine forest to sparse larch forest to fields of flowers and views east to Cape Horn and Ladies Pass, gaining 1900 feet in 1½ miles, to crest at 6700 feet on a sharp ridge, then dropping abruptly to little Carter Lake, 6200 feet. The trail disappears in meadows; cross a small stream and proceed straight ahead, keeping the lake to the left, passing marshy camps strongly favored by mosquitoes and no-see-ums. At this point, the trail reappears. Cross another small creek to the Painter Creek trail intersection, 2 miles from Index Creek (11¾ miles from the road-end), elevation 6200 feet.

Recross the small creek and rapidly descend lush meadows. In ¼ mile, just before crossing Painter Creek, are good camps. At ½ mile below the lake the trail flattens to traverse rich meadows and brushy clearings. The way crosses Painter Creek four more times and passes many camps before meeting The Badlands trail (Hike 19) at 5½ miles from Carter Lake.

The Painter valley narrows and the path is cleverly laced between cliffs in a series of traverses and drops for 2½ miles before reaching South Fork Chiwaukum Creek, which must be forded to close the loop 7½ miles from Carter Lake, a total of 18¾ miles from the start. The familiar Chiwaukum River is followed for the final 5½ miles back to the starting point.

For a longer loop, skip Index Creek, continue on the South Fork Chiwaukum trail to Ladies Pass, and there turn left on Icicle Ridge trail to Painter Creek, a journey of 5 to 6 days with several thousand feet more elevation gain but only some 6 more miles.

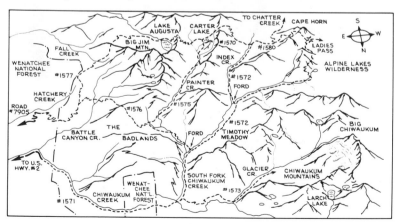

ICICLE RIDGE

Round trip to Lake Augusta 36
  miles
Allow 3–4 days
High point 7029 feet
Elevation gain 8000 feet in, 2500
  feet out

Hikable (in part) May through
  mid-October
USGS Leavenworth and
  Chiwaukum Mountains

Any hiker of spirit cannot but yearn to set out from the edge of Leavenworth, climb to the crest of Icicle Ridge, and walk the skyline to Big Jim Mountain and Lake Augusta and onward to Ladies Pass, Snowgrass Mountain, and Frosty Pass. Many hikers do indeed glory in the meadows and lakes of the latter part of Icicle Ridge trail. However, the earlier stretch, though just as scenic and paradoxically much wilder, is bone-dry after the end of snowmelt and thus rarely hiked. All the better for solitude, and not too thirsty if done when patches of snow linger.

The disaster threatening this splendid ridge is—as everywhere hereabout—the Northern Pacific Land Grant. Though Longview Fiber never built any railroads, it has acquired several grant sections on the ridge and plans to build a logging road that would ruin the trail and open the fragile crest to motorized havoc. If a direct switchbacking access is not permitted, one will contour around from farther up Icicle Creek, sparing the trail yet still attracting fun machines to lonesome highlands. Any innocent who supposes the Alpine Lakes Wilderness is "complete" had better think again.

From US 2 on the west side of Leavenworth drive south 1.4 miles on Icicle Creek road, go right on a bit of old highway, and in .1 mile find Icicle Ridge trail No. 1570, elevation 1200 feet.

The start truly tests hikers, climbing 1600 feet in 2 miles to the ridge crest and continuing to climb as the crest aims for the sky. At 6 miles, 5200 feet, the angle eases somewhat, though by no means becoming flat.

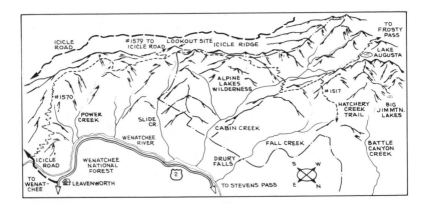

Mount Stuart Range from Icicle Ridge trail

Views begin and at 8 miles meadows. At 9 miles the way passes the Fourth of July Creek trail (Hike 26) and the site of Icicle Ridge Lookout, 7029 feet, highest point of the route. Really thirsty hikers may be interested to learn that the lookout used to fetch water from a small spring about 1400 vertical feet down the trail from his cabin.

Going down more than up, the ridge trail follows the crest another 2½ miles before dropping to Cabin Creek at 13 miles, 5000 feet, and the first certain all-summer water. The way ascends from the valley to a meadowy ridge paralleling Icicle Ridge (whose crest is not regained until Ladies Pass), at 16½ miles, 6700 feet, passes Hatchery Creek trail (Hike 19), and at 18 miles attains Lake Augusta, 6854 feet.

The Icicle Ridge trail proceeds over two high passes (Hikes 19 and 20), rounds a shoulder of Cape Horn to Ladies Pass, and ends at Frosty Pass (Hike 36), 24 miles from that spirited beginning.

Gnome Tarn and Prusik Peak

22 ENCHANTMENT LAKES

**Round trip to Snow Lakes 13½
miles
Allow 2 days
High point 5415 feet
Elevation gain 3800 feet
Hikable July through October
USGS Mt. Stuart and Liberty**

**Round trip to Lower
Enchantment Lakes 20 miles
Allow 3–4 days
High point 7000 feet
Elevation gain 5400 feet
Hikable late July through
mid-October**

A legendary group of lakes in rock basins over 7000 feet high amid the
Cashmere Crags of the Stuart Range; one of the most famous places in
the Cascade Mountains. Large lakes, small ponds, gigantic slabs of ice-
polished granite, flower gardens, heather meadows, trees gnarled and
twisted by the elements, waterfalls, snowfields, and glaciers. Visit in
summer for flowers, in late September to see the autumn gold of larch.

This is not a trip for beginners. The way is long, steep, and grueling. A
strong hiker needs at least 12 hours to reach the high lakes. The average
hiker takes 2 days. The rest never make it.

It also is not a trip for hermits. The scene is mobbed from early summer, when the snow is still deep, until late fall, when it's piling up again.
It's mobbed on holidays, mobbed on weekends, mobbed in midweek.

If you decide to come anyhow, be prepared to obey as stringent a moral
code as any in American wilderness. The fragility of the vegetation requires it. So does the population density. Motorcycles were the first
superconsumers to be prohibited. Then came horses. —And then,
dogs—do not expect law-abiding hikers to accept your excuse that "Gee, I
never go no place without good ol' Slasher." Bring a stove—wood fires are
banned. Camp on bare ground at established sites. Look for those less
used, away from the main trail. Use toilets where provided. Boil your water. Walk on rock or snow rather than plants. Limit party size to six. If
you can't live with all that, do without the hike.

Drive US 2 east from Stevens Pass to Leavenworth. On the west out-

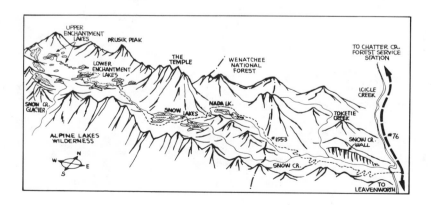

Glacier-polished rock and Lake Viviane

skirts of town turn south on Icicle Creek road. At 4 miles turn left into the Snow Lakes trail parking area, elevation 1600 feet.

Snow Lakes trail No. 1553 crosses the river and immediately starts up—and up. The way switchbacks upward in forest, with views in the early part to the granite cliffs of Snow Creek Wall. Small camps at approximately 2 miles, 2800 feet, offer a break in the journey for parties with heavy packs or not too much energy and wishing to make the approach in easy stages. At 5½ miles is Nada Lake, 5000 feet, and good camps. At 6¾ miles the trail passes between the two Snow Lakes at 5415 feet. For camping here, find sites to the left at the lower lake and all the way around the left side of the upper lake to where the trail finally starts up. To the north rises 8292-foot Temple and to the south 8364-foot Mt. McClellan. All beginners and most average hikers find this far enough, and these lakes magnificent enough—as indeed they are, but it just happens their beauty can't hold a candle to what lies above.

To continue to the Enchantments, cross the low dam between the two lakes. Pause to note this rather weird interference with nature: like a bathtub, water is drained through a hole in the bottom of the upper lake (which thus has a fluctuating shoreline) and is used to guarantee a pure intake for the Leavenworth Fish Hatchery; probably few people imagined, when the project was perpetrated back in the 1930s, that Snow Lakes would become as popular as they are.

Follow the trail winding along the left shore. At the south end cross the inlet stream and proceed up Snow Creek, climbing into granite country.

The area was discovered by A. H. Sylvester, a topographer for the U.S. Geological Survey for some 13 years and then, from 1908 to 1931, supervisor of Wenatchee National Forest. In his years of exploring he placed thousands of names on maps of the West. "Enchantment" expressed his reaction—and that of all who have followed. The one name covered everything until climbers arrived in the late 1940s and began assigning vivid names to "The Crags." Then came Bill and Peg Stark, who over many years drew on various mythologies to name the lakes and other features. A lake and its swordlike rock peninsula became Lake Viviane and Excalibur Rock. Other lakes and tarns they called Rune, Talisman, Valkyrie, Leprechaun, Naiad, Lorelei, Dryad, Pixie, Gnome, Brisingamen, Brynhild, Reginleif, Sprite, and Titania. And there is Troll Sink (a pond), Valhalla Cirque, Tanglewood, and many more.

Lower Enchantment Basin, at 7000 feet, is friendliest. Upper Enchantment Basin, at 7500 feet, has desolate splendor. Some of its lakes are clear and some are jade-colored by rock milk and some are frozen solid all summer. When Sylvester was here—not all that long ago—nearly the whole basin was occupied by the Snow Creek Glacier.

23 LAKE CAROLINE

Round trip 11 miles	**Hikable mid-July through**
Hiking time 8 hours	**October**
High point 6190 feet	**One day or backpack**
Elevation gain 2870 feet	**USGS Chiwaukum Mountains**

Another delightful spot of the Alpine Lakes Wilderness, a high tree-lined lake, meadows, and a wealth of rocky cliffs. A special treat is the great north face of 9415-foot Mt. Stuart, seen from close enough to make out crevasses in the hanging glaciers.

The trail to Lake Caroline crosses the checkerboard ownership inherited from the railroad land grants. The present owners are cutting their land and in the first 1½ miles the trail is disrupted in several places.

Drive US 2 east from Stevens Pass to Leavenworth. On the west outskirts of town turn south on Icicle Creek road. At 8.5 miles turn left across a bridge on road No. 7601 up Eightmile Creek, climbing steeply 3 miles to the trailhead, elevation 3320 feet. Eightmile Lake trail No. 1552, on the uphill side of the road, is clearly signed.

The trail ascends moderately, following Eightmile Creek, with about ½ mile of road-walking. At 2½ miles the way reaches Little Eightmile Lake, 4400 feet, and a junction. The left fork goes another ½ mile up the valley to 4641-foot Eightmile Lake and good camps. The lake is ringed by woods but awesome rock walls rise far above the trees.

The right fork climbs an endless series of switchbacks (hot and thirsty on sunny days) from the valley, first in timber, then emerging into meadows. The labor is rewarded by steadily improving views to the jagged spires of the Stuart Range and finally the tall thrust of Mt. Stuart itself. At 5½ miles, the alpine basin of Lake Caroline, 6190 feet. The most attractive campsites are ½ mile farther and 200 feet higher at Little Lake Caroline, surrounded by meadows.

The best is yet to come. The 2-mile hike to 7200-foot Windy Pass, on

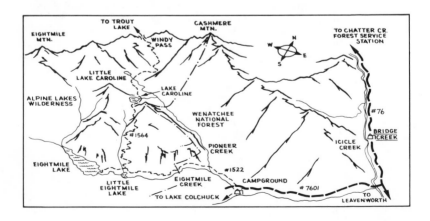

Lake Caroline and Cashmere Mountain

good trail amid flowers and larches, is an absolute must. For broader views, walk the ridge toward 8501-foot Cashmere Mountain—but don't try for the summit; the last pitches are strictly for climbers.

An alternate return route (not too practical unless one can hitch a ride back to the car) can be made by going 8 miles from Windy Pass down Trout Creek to the Chatter Creek Guard Station. This trail passes through a mile of clearcuts on more railroad grant land.

To preserve vegetation, campers are asked to use only established campsites.

Eightmile road   Old: 2412
                     New: 7601

24   LAKE STUART– COLCHUCK LAKE

Round trip to Colchuck Lake 9
  miles
Hiking time 8 hours
High point 5570 feet
Elevation gain 2000 feet
Hikable mid-July through
  October
One day or backpack
USGS Chiwaukum Mountains and
  Mt. Stuart

Round trip to Lake Stuart 9 miles
Hiking time 7 hours
High point 5064 feet
Elevation gain 1500 feet

Two large lakes amid alpine forests and granite cliffs of the Stuart
Range. Hike to emerald waters of Colchuck Lake and contemplate towering crags above, decorated with two small glaciers. Or, to cure itchy feet,
visit nearby Lake Stuart. Or, if it's peace and quiet you want, don't come
here at all because this is the most heavily used trail and lake system in
the vicinity—even more so than the Enchantments!

From Icicle Creek road (Hike 23) drive 4 miles on road No. 7601 to the
trailhead, elevation 3540 feet. Find Lake Stuart–Colchuck Lake trail
No. 1599 at a sharp turn of the road on the creek side.

The trail parallels Mountaineer Creek on a constant upward grade for
1 mile, then switchbacks up the steepening valley to a junction at 2½
miles, 4600 feet.

The left trail (a rough path) crosses Mountaineer Creek and ascends
with many switchbacks, in open forest among numerous granite knolls,
along the cascading waters of East Fork Mountaineer Creek. During the
final ¼ mile the way bypasses a waterfall, leaves the creek, and comes to
a tiny, almost landlocked lagoon of Colchuck Lake, 5570 feet, 4½ miles.
Incredibly, this lovely blue-green lake, like others in the area, is drained

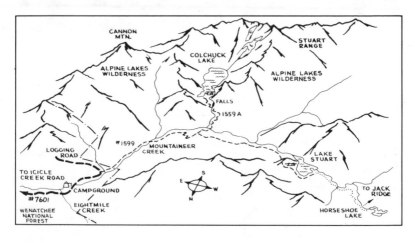

Mount Stuart from Lake Stuart

for use by the Icicle Irrigation District. Camping all the way around the right side of the lake. **Note:** Dogs are not allowed on this trail.

The right trail (notorious as probably the doggiest in the Cascades) proceeds gently up the main fork of Mountaineer Creek to the wooded shores, clear blue water, and tall cliffs of Lake Stuart, 5064 feet, 4½ miles. Campsites near the point where the trail first reaches the lake. Follow the trail ¾ mile beyond the lake to a marshy meadow under the towering cliffs of Mt. Stuart. Beyond lies *wild* wilderness, brushy and craggy, mean and dangerous; Horseshoe Lake and Jack Ridge are strictly for the super-doughty.

To preserve the vegetation, campers are asked to use established sites.

Eightmile road	Old:	2412	Old:	2412A
	New:	7601	New:	7601

25   AASGARD PASS

Round trip to lower Enchantment Lakes 15 miles
Allow 3–4 days
High point 7750 feet
Elevation gain 4410 feet in, 670 feet out

Scrambleable August through mid-September
USGS Chiwaukum Mountains and Mt. Stuart

Three things often are said to be radically wrong with the Snow Lakes route to the Enchantments (Hike 22): too many miles and too much elevation and, when you get there, too many people. A myth has it that the Colchuck Lake approach, pioneered by climbers aiming at peaks of the Dragontail group, is an easy shortcut and has solitude to boot. Don't believe it. Four things are terribly wrong with the entry via Aasgard Pass: It's not easy; actually it's a climbers' route, usually requiring ice ax, sometimes rope and crampons, and in early summer the ability to recognize avalanche instability. It's dangerous, not only from falling off cliffs or slippery boulders or snowfields or from being fallen upon by snow or rock, but also from summer storms that at 7500 feet can be distinctly hypothermic and from summer snowfalls that can make the already difficult descent of boulder fields a very long nightmare. It's not esthetic — instead of ascending ritually and respectfully from the picturesque lower

Barren slopes and upper Enchantment Lakes

basin to the austere upper basin and at last to the cold snows and stern stones of Aasgard, one does it all backward, like starting with the ice cream and working through the meatballs and potatoes to the soup. Finally, when you get to the Enchantments the mob is already there, never fear.

Why, then, is the route in this book? As a warning against myths. To save the innocent from being suckered in by "the easy way to the Enchantments." Also to quash the faddy notion this is the classy and sassy way, the route of the big kids. For anyone it's a tasteless route. For hikers lacking climbing equipment and training it's a route silly to the point of suicidal.

If determined to be tasteless and silly, drive to the Lake Stuart–Colchuck Lake trailhead, elevation 3540 feet, and hike 4½ miles to Colchuck Lake, 5570 feet (Hike 24).

Round the shore to the right, to a camping area where formal trail ends and boulder-hopping begins. Ascend under the Colchuck Glacier on the side of Colchuck Peak, over talus from Colchuck Col, and beneath Dragontail Peak to slopes below Aasgard Pass.

The ascent is the next thing to vertical, gaining 2200 feet in ¾ mile on small rocks that slide under the boot and large rocks that in rain or snow the boot skids on. Watch for cairns piled up by the Forest Service, a practice generally not accepted in the wilderness but necessary here to keep neophytes from straying into the cliffs. About two-thirds of the way, cross to the right under a knot of trees and rocks and follow cairns over a small stream and a snowfield to the pass, 7750 feet.

You and your heavy pack are now at a nobly arctic and splendidly scenic lunch stop and climactic turnaround point for hikers exploring (with rucksack loads only) upward from camps in the comfort of the lower basin. However, for you to enjoy a cozy night you must traverse the upper basin, a joy to the eye but pleasantly campable only in the most benign conditions, and descend past the meatballs to the potatoes and, in grim weather, even to the soup. But be of good cheer. You don't *have* to climb back to Aasgard in that raging storm. As more than one "shortcut" party has learned, via Snow Creek trail and road it's only 18 miles back to your car.

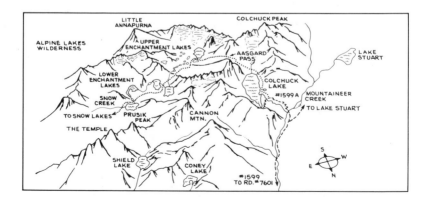

Cashmere Mountain from Fourth of July Creek trail

ICICLE CREEK
Alpine Lakes Wilderness

 FOURTH OF JULY CREEK

Round trip 13 miles
Hiking time 8 hours
High point 7000 feet
Elevation gain 4600 feet

Hikable May (in part) through
October
USGS Chiwaukum Mountains

In all the Icicle country the Fourth of July trail is the best day hike to high views of Mt. Stuart, Mt. Cashmere, the meadowy-craggy length of Icicle Ridge, and bulky ramparts of the Chiwaukum Mountains. If the

4600 feet all the way to the old lookout site exceed the available muscle power, panoramas are proportionately rewarding three-quarters or even halfway up, and this much of the trail, on a southerly exposure as it is, can be done before June, when the floral display of this rainshadow side of the Cascades is in its best weeks of the year.

Drive US 2 to Leavenworth. On the west outskirts of town turn south on the Icicle Creek road. At 8.5 miles pass Eightmile Creek junction and at 9.4 miles find a small paved parking area and Fourth of July trail No. 1579, elevation 2400 feet.

The trailhead sign gives the distance as 5 miles; it feels like 7 or 8; we've compromised on 6. The trail wastes little time getting down to business, in ¼ mile crossing the creek (the last certain water) and addressing a series of short switchbacks that will numb your mind if you try to count them. Focus instead on the flowers and on the views that begin as window glimpses and grow to wide screen, especially to 8501-foot Cashmere Mountain directly across the Icicle valley.

A mile below the ridge crest the way quits the zigzag and begins a traversing ascent eastward. At about 5400 feet is a spring where the fire lookout used to come for water, though maybe not by summer's end. Due to the scarcity of water on this sunny south slope, rattlesnakes gather from miles around to have a sip and cool off in the grass and mud, so don't be too greedy.

At 6800 feet, about 6 miles, the path attains the crest and joins Icicle Ridge trail No. 1570 (Hike 21). Ascend a final ¼ mile to the lookout site, 7000 feet. The cabin was perched atop a rock thumb and was reached by ladder. Cabin and ladder are gone and the thumb is difficult. Never mind—the view from the bottom is as good as from the top.

Icicle Creek road   Old: 2451
                       New: 76

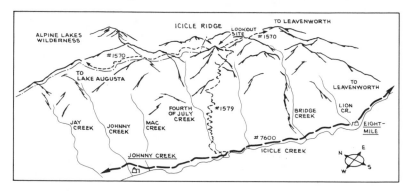

27 TROUT CREEK– JACK CREEK LOOP

Loop trip 11¾ miles
Hiking time 7 hours
High point 5800 feet
Elevation gain 3100 feet

Hikable mid-July through
mid-October
One day or backpack
USGS Chiwaukum Mountains

The miles of beautiful virgin forest can be savored on up-and-back hikes along either of the valley trails. However, for no greater expenditure of time and energy they can be connected in a loop that has a historically interesting middle section. To wit, while conservationists were campaigning to create an Alpine Lakes Wilderness, the heirs of the Northern Pacific Land Grant were logging as fast as they could to reduce the wilderness to the smallest possible size. Which is to say, the middle of the loop is in clearcuts. To discourage travelers from viewing the evidence, the Forest Service doesn't maintain the Trout Creek trail very enthusiastically, leaving lots of logs to crawl over and much water to leap across.

Drive US 2 to Leavenworth. On the west outskirts of town turn south on the Icicle Creek road 12.9 miles on pavement, 2.6 miles on dirt, and just past the Information Center find Jack Creek trailhead No. 1558, elevation 2700 feet.

The trail drops to cross Icicle Creek and wanders a pretty ¼ mile upstream. At a picnic area–campsite turn uphill from the riverside path to a junction at ½ mile, 3100 feet. The right fork is the return leg of the loop along Jack Creek; go left on Trout Creek trail No. 1555. (The loop is recommended in this direction because crucial junctions are not marked to be easily seen coming the other way.)

Good trail ascends steadily 2 miles—to a logging road, where are spent the next 1½ miles enjoying views (which disappear in time) of Icicle Ridge to the south and Eightmile Mountain ahead, but also gnashing teeth at the stumps. High on the side of the valley, trudge from clearcut to clearcut. At the first two road junctions stay left. At the third go right,

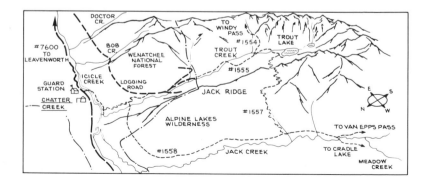

Bridge over Icicle Creek on the Jack Creek trail

descending the clearcut into forest and at 3½ miles entering the Alpine Lakes Wilderness.

The nearly flat trail fords Trout Creek twice and at 4½ miles, 4600 feet, intersects trail No. 1554; for a great sidetrip climb 2½ miles to Windy Pass above Lake Caroline (Hike 23). A final ½ mile leads to a junction at Trout Lake, 4800 feet. Campsites are straight ahead on the shore. The loop trail crosses the creek, climbs 1½ miles to the forested crest of a ridge, 5800 feet, and switchbacks down to the Jack Creek trail at 8½ miles, 3700 feet.

The loop is closed with 3¼ miles on good horse trail down Jack Creek in virgin forests. Enjoy them. Enjoy the peace and quiet. Forget the former teeth-gnashing and laugh a little. Had the Forest Service plan been accepted, there would not have been a single, unified Alpine Lakes Wilderness but two wildernesses, separated by a road that would have let trucks and tourists drive from Icicle Creek up Jack Creek, over Van Epps Pass, and down to the Cle Elum River road.

Icicle Creek road   Old: 2512
                            New: 7600

28   CHATTER CREEK–
LAKE EDNA

Round trip to Chatter Creek Basin
5 miles
Hiking time 3 hours
High point 5300 feet
Elevation gain 2300 feet
Hikable July through
mid-September
One day or backpack
USGS Chiwaukum Mountains

Round trip to Lake Edna 11½
miles
Hiking time 8 hours
High point 6750 feet
Elevation gain 3750 feet
Hikable mid-July through
mid-September

The Chatter Creek trail is a quick, though by no means easy, way to the much-beloved alpine realm of "Mormon Ladies Lakes," by legend (but not historical fact) named for the many wives of Brigham Young. However, the creek's headwaters cirque beneath rugged walls of Grindstone Mountain is delight enough for a day, and a spectacular highland traverse leads to Lake Edna, lonesomest and perhaps the prettiest of the ladies.

Drive US 2 to Leavenworth. On the west outskirts of town turn south on Icicle Creek road 15.8 miles, .3 mile past Chatter Creek Campground, and go off right .1 mile on the sideroad to Chatter Creek trail No. 1580, elevation 3000 feet.

The trail starts on an old road through a brushy clearcut, in 100 yards splitting; go right. In ¼ mile the road quits and, after passing a hunters' camp at the end of the logging, the trail goes to work, climbing open forest along Chatter Creek 1400 feet in the next 1¼ miles, then crossing the creek and rounding a corner to enter the upper, hanging valley. In a final ½ mile the steepness of the angle relents and the path levels to enter the open basin. Near timberline at 2½ miles, 5300 feet, a little ex-

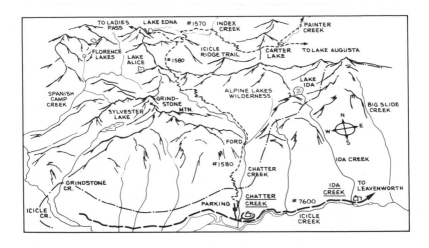

Cashmere Mountain from upper Chatter Creek trail

ploration leads to two small campsites, scenic spots for day hikers to eat their peanut-butter-and-jelly sandwiches while gazing over the Icicle valley to Trout Creek and Eightmile Mountain and over Jack Ridge to Blackjack Ridge and Bootjack Mountain.

The trail switchbacks steeply across a 6700-foot rubble shoulder of Grindstone Mountain at 3½ miles, descends to glorious headwater meadows of Index Creek and several campsites, elevation 6400 feet. Follow rock cairns and faint trail left over a boulder field, contouring to a second, larger basin below Cape Horn, where the trail disappears. Descend to a large cairn at the base of the meadow, cross a small stream, then head uphill through a band of trees to an open rib. Hike up the rib to the edge of an upper basin, then go to the right, crossing another small stream, and scramble straight uphill and follow a now-visible boot path the final last push to reach the Icicle Ridge trail No. 1570 (Hike 21) at 5½ miles.

Go left in meadows, over buttresses of ice-polished-and-gouged rock, to snowy-stony, austerely beautiful Lake Edna, 5¾ miles, 6735 feet. The camps are small and naked to the storm winds that swirl around the summit of Cape Horn, close above, but in a calm summer night, wonderful for quiet dreams.

Icicle Creek road   Old: 2512
                            New: 7600

Icicle Ridge from Bootjack Mountain

ICICLE CREEK
Alpine Lakes Wilderness

BLACKJACK RIDGE

Round trip to open meadows 6
  miles
Hiking time 5 hours
High point 6100 feet
Elevation gain 3250 feet

Hikable mid-July through
  mid-September
One day or backpack
USGS Chiwaukum Mountains

Views are superb over the Icicle valley to Icicle Ridge and Grindstone Mountain, to the isolated mass of Cashmere Mountain and the impressive northwest face of Mt. Stuart, and to the lonesome length of Sixtysix Hundred Ridge. There is solitude, too, for reasons: The trail is extremely steep and fails to hold hard-won elevation but goes upsy-downsy along the ridge, spots level enough for a sleeping bag are few, and water is scarcer yet. If the trail is combined in a loop with the Snowall–Cradle Lake trip (Hike 33), it is most wisely chosen as the exit rather than the entry. This is an option reserved for expert route finders only; the trail disappears in Pablo Creek Basin.

Drive US 2 to Leavenworth. On the west outskirts of town turn south on the Icicle Creek road 19.2 miles to just before the crossing of Black Pine Creek, 300 feet before a horse-loading ramp, and on the uphill side of the road find trail No. 1565, elevation 2850 feet. (No trailhead sign in 1985; if you reach the end of the Icicle Road, you've gone ¼ mile too far.)

The trail starts in an area of selective logging (all the big, beautiful trees selected, otherwise known as "high-grading") but in ¼ mile enters the Alpine Lakes Wilderness and commences switchbacks that seem steeper at each turn and appear unlikely ever to end this side of the moon. However, in 2¾ miles the ascent gentles in open meadows atop Blackjack Ridge. The trail skims through fragile flowers to a high point of 6100 feet, 3 miles, on the shoulder of 6789-foot Bootjack Mountain. Here is the first view of the great wall of Mt. Stuart and a proper place for day hikers to suck their dusty canteens before heading home.

Day hikers should be satisfied with looking into the green basin below the 6100-foot shoulder of Bootjack Mountain. However, if after climbing 3300 feet, there is still energy left, follow the ridge upward on a faint foot trail through forest and meadows with expanding views. The ridge is blocked twice by rocky outcrops. Go right of the first pyramid shaped rock and left of the second jumbled mess to the rocky summit of 6789-foot Bootjack. The final 70 feet takes a bit of scramble that is generally not recommended for hikers without mountaineering experience.

Icicle Creek road   Old: 2512
                                New: 7600

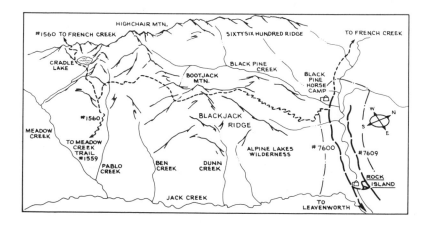

30   ICICLE CREEK

Round trip to Josephine Lake 22½ miles
Allow 2–3 days
High point 4681 feet
Elevation gain 1780 feet

Hikable July through mid-October
USGS Chiwaukum Mountains and Stevens Pass

The Icicle Creek trail is the main arterial of the northeast sector of the Alpine Lakes Wilderness. It leads to almost everywhere, hooks up tributary trails for all manner of loops, in itself is a splendid route through deep forest to deep blue waters of Josephine Lake and gardens of the Cascade Crest, and has frequent pleasant camps beside the stream that make the lower stretches extremely popular with families introducing children to backpacking. In the upper stretches the maintenance is spotty, and at places hikers must burrow through over-the-head brush.

Drive US 2 to Leavenworth. On the west outskirts of town turn south on the Icicle Creek road 17.5 miles to a split at Rock Island Campground. Go left 1.9 miles on road No. 7600 to the end and Icicle Creek trailhead No. 1551, elevation 2900 feet.

The trail rolls through quiet forest 1¼ miles to super-popular French Creek Camp, crosses French Creek to more campsites and a junction with French Creek trail (Hike 31). Continue along the Icicle to the next junction, 1½ miles, with the French Ridge trail (Hike 35). A scant ½ mile beyond, pass the Frosty Creek–Wildhorse trail (Hike 36). Near 4 miles is the unsigned start of the Doughgod Creek trail, shown on maps but long abandoned and practically inaccessible across unbridged Icicle Creek.

At 4½ miles pass a large camp and cross Icicle Creek on a bridge to further camps, 3080 feet, ascend briefly, cross two very brushy avalanche paths, and at a third campsite come to the Leland Creek junction, 6 miles, 3240 feet (camps on both sides of Icicle Creek but no trace of vanished Bark Cabin), and the takeoff for Hikes 37, 38, and 39.

At 7½ miles, 3400 feet, something dramatic happens. To here the valley has been wide and the floor virtually flat, the trail the next thing to level, and the creek generally quiet, with many delicious swimming

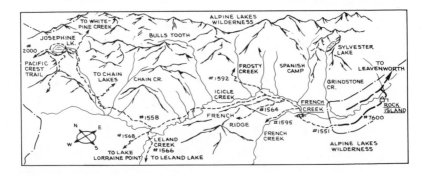

pools. But here, where in ancient times lesser glaciers gathered into one mighty glacier, performing the usual job of grinding the valley down at the heel, the trail must climb, and it does, switchbacking a steep step upward into a narrower hanging valley, at 8½ miles, 3800 feet, passing Chain Lakes trail (Hike 12).

The upper valley attained, the trail flattens a bit, passing another camp in the woods, recrossing Icicle Creek at 9 miles, and at 10½ miles reaching the Whitepine trail, 4400 feet. At last the way emerges into subalpine meadows on a final climb to the cirque of Josephine Lake, 11¼ miles, 4681 feet, and much-used camps.

A final ¾-mile ascent of heather meadows reaches the end of the Icicle Creek trail at the Pacific Crest Trail, 5000 feet. Should a one-way hike be the party's intent, an easy 4 miles lead to Stevens Pass (Hike 11).

Icicle Creek road   Old: 2512
                              New: 7600

Cloudy day along upper Icicle Creek trail

31   FRENCH CREEK

Round trip to Meadow Creek Pass
  24 miles
Allow 2–3 days
High point 5320 feet
Elevation gain 2400 feet plus
  many ups and downs

Hikable July through
  mid-October
USGS Chiwaukum Mountains,
  Stevens Pass, The Cradle

When the famous valleys grow crowded, obscure valleys grow all the more appealing. French Creek has green forests and white water and cozy camps to keep hikers smiling quietly in their solitude. However, the trail isn't totally lonesome because it does have a degree of fame as an access to alpine lakes and meadows.

Drive the Icicle Creek road to the end, elevation 2900 feet, and hike the Icicle Creek trail 1¼ miles to French Creek trail No. 1595, 2900 feet (Hike 30).

French Creek

Also signed "Backdoor Trail," the way follows the north bank of the creek. At about 3 miles (from the Icicle road) admire the monstrous swath of an avalanche that swept down the opposite ridge, across the valley bottom, and 200 feet up this side of the valley to the trail. *There* was a spectacle that would have made the day for a party of cross-country skiers or snowshoers.

At 3¾ miles pass a nice (and popular) campsite. At 5 miles is the south end of French Ridge and the takeoff of Backdoor Trail No. 1564A, presumably so named to avoid confusion with the north end of the same trail, though at that end it's called "French Ridge Trail" (Hike 32). At 6 miles are the confluence of French and Snowall Creeks, another good camp, and the start of Cradle Lake trail No. 1560 (Hike 33).

At 7¼ miles are a camp and a difficult crossing of Klonaqua Creek. Small logs upstream may perhaps be scooted; otherwise the feet must be got wet, and the knees, and possibly the hips. That done, pass the start of Klonaqua Lakes trail No. 1563 (Hike 34), 3700 feet. Since that's the destination of nearly everyone who travels the French Creek trail, the solitude now deepens, down in the shadowy forest where rarely is the contemplation of greenery disturbed by glimpses of high snowfields and peaks or sky.

Henceforth the path is populated by more (almost) horses than people and is typically mudholed and root tangled. At 11 miles pass Paddy-Go-Easy Pass trail No. 1595 (Hikes 71 and 72), which crosses the ridge to the Cle Elum River valley. At 12 miles the trail tops out on the wooded flat of Meadow Creek Pass, 5320 feet, in itself not much of a destination, but the way continues as Meadow Creek trail No. 1559, dropping past a sidetrail to Pablo Basin and Cradle Lake (a loop! a loop!) to Jack Creek and on down to the Icicle road (another loop!).

Icicle Creek road   Old: 2512
                              New: 7600

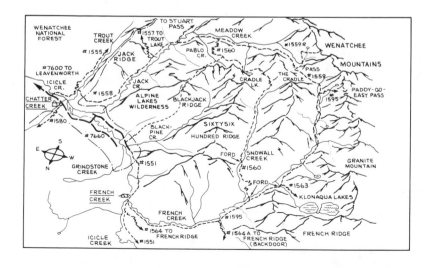

32 TURQUOISE LAKE

Round trip 17 miles
Allow 2–3 days
High point 6000 feet
Elevation gain 3600 feet in, 900 feet out

Hikable mid-July through mid-September
USGS Stevens Pass, Chiwaukum Mountains, The Cradle

When all the easy trails fill up with happy faces, mean and nasty trails grow more attractive, especially when the goal is a sparkling lake, ⅓

Turquoise Lake

mile long, tucked in a narrow cirque so difficult to reach that crowds are too thin to deserve the name.

Drive the Icicle Creek road to the end, elevation 2900 feet, and hike the Icicle Creek and French Creek trails to the takeoff of the Backdoor Trail, here signed only "French Ridge Trail," at 3300 feet, 5 miles from the Icicle Creek road (Hike 31).

Because the hike is too strenuous for most folks to do in a day and there is no dependable water from French Creek nearly to the lake, the best plan is to camp at the inviting spot beside the creek at 3¾ miles (from the road) and set out very early next morning carrying quarts of water.

The reason for suggesting a very early start becomes apparent as the trail starts steep and gets steeper, switchbacking up a parched, south-facing slope with little shade and gaining 1500 feet in what is officially measured as 1 mile, though a person is likely to feel a zero ought to be added on. Quitting the zigzags but not the climbing, the way sidehills east a long ½ mile into a small basin of subalpine trees and flowers, but no water after the snow goes. Here is an unmarked junction, 5450 feet.

The French Ridge trail proceeds straight ahead in meadows 1½ miles to the site of the old French Ridge Lookout (Hike 35). A rough way trail sets out northward over French Ridge to Lake Cuitin.

Go left, southwesterly, on the unsigned trail to Turquoise Lake. After a nice bit to sucker you in, the trouble begins. The way climbs 500 feet more to swing around a spur of French Ridge, then loses the 500 feet into the valley of a nameless tributary of French Creek; a delightful camp here, and water. Another 400 feet are lost getting around cliffs and rockslides of another spur ridge and 500 feet are regained reaching meager camps at the outlet of Turquoise Lake, 5465 feet, about 8½ miles from the road. One can only hope the fishing is worth it.

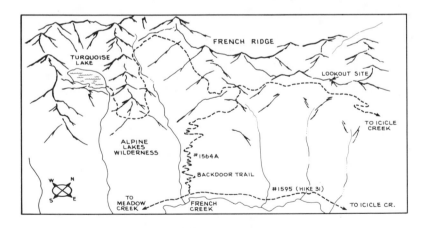

33 SNOWALL CREEK– CRADLE LAKE

Round trip 26 miles
Allow 2–3 days
High point 6300 feet
Elevation gain 3400 feet

Hikable August through
September
USGS Chiwaukum Mountains,
Stevens Pass, The Cradle

Another thing, aside from many miles and much elevation gain, that contributes to lonesomeness is deep, swift water lacking bridge or foot-log. Were it not for two such tests of courage, the flower gardens of upper Snowall Creek surely would be thronged. Should you be unlucky and find a considerable population, try again earlier in summer when the snow-melt is flooding.

Drive the Icicle Creek road to the end, elevation 2900 feet, and hike the Icicle Creek and French Creek trails to the start of Snowall Creek–Cradle Lake trail No. 1560 at 3550 feet, 6 miles from the road (Hike 31).

Right off the bat there's a ford of French Creek, usually only knee-deep in August, and not so wide and cold but what you might still be able to feel your toes when you reach the far bank. Switchbacks gain 1000 feet in 2 miles to a second ford, of Snowall Creek, deeper and swifter than the first; a stout pole is a help; short people should be tied to a rope and fitted with scuba gear.

The angle of ascent lies back as the way crosses numerous flower-rich meadows, some dry and some wet for an optimum display of species. Views open to walls of 7467-foot Cradle and snows on ridges at the valley head. At 2½ miles pass a well-used camp and at 4¾ miles enter a meadow ½ mile long, dominated in August by myriad blossoms of Merten's bluebells (many are pinkbells).

The trip now seems to have come to an abrupt end, the amphitheater of cliffs curving in a horseshoe from The Cradle to Highchair Mountain plainly a cul de sac. However, from the far side of the meadow, 5000 feet, the trail zigs and zags and zags and zigs, finding an improbable cleft in the valley wall and climbing to a scenic pass, 6300 feet, in the ridge from Highchair. In ¼ mile more drop to the flowers rimming Cradle Lake,

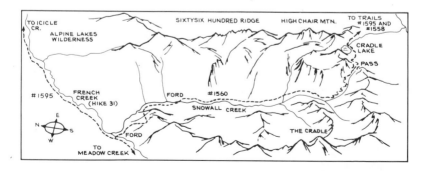

Cradle Lake

6200 feet, 13 miles from the Icicle road—which is to say, 13 miles the way *you* came.

Are there more people in the lake camps than you expected? That's because there's a shorter approach, via Pablo and Jack Creeks (a loop!). So maybe you should've stopped amid the bluebells of Snowall Creek, and a lovely place to stop it is.

34 KLONAQUA LAKES

Round trip 19 miles
Allow 2–3 days
High point 5300 feet
Elevation gain 2400 feet in, 200
 feet out

Hikable mid-July through
 mid-October
USGS Chiwaukum Mountains,
 Stevens Pass, The Cradle

Whatever sort of "aqua" is "klon," the two lakes of that name are among the largest splashes of blue on maps of the eastern Alpine Lakes Wilderness, and there's nothing like blue on a map to draw gangs of fishing poles, people attached. The views are as spectacular as the blueness of the aqua, up bare cliffs to snowy summits of Granite Mountain. Though, in fact, the blue of the lower lake is usually ice-white until mid-July, and of the upper until August, the trip is so popular and sections of the path so rooty and rocky, the trail is signed "hiker only," no horses allowed.

Drive the Icicle Creek road to the end, elevation 2900 feet, and hike Icicle Creek and French Creek trails to a difficult ford of Klonaqua Creek and the start of Klonaqua Lakes trail No. 1563 at 3700 feet, 7¼ miles from the road (Hike 31).

The trail sets right out to do its job of climbing to the fish, half the way in sight and sound of the creek, then switchbacking away into huge boulders, with several glimpses of a mighty waterfall from the cirque. At about 2 miles the path briefly levels at a camp, then ascends above a rockslide to a ridge crest at 5300 feet and drops to lower Klonaqua Lake, 5090 feet, 9½ miles from the road.

Clumps of trees and patches of huckleberries and heather shore the lake, whose outlet was dammed in the dim past by the Icicle Irrigation District (for use during drought years), raising the level some 5 feet. Above the basin rise rugged summits of 7144-foot Granite Mountain.

To reach the upper lake, 5187 feet, take the fishermen's path steeply

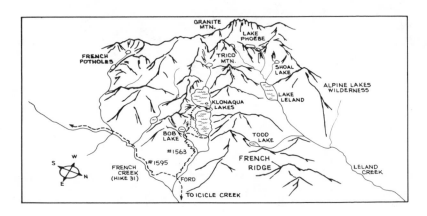

from the outlet, around the left side of the lake, a scant 1 mile to the narrow isthmus between the two.

Within conceivable exploring range of camps here are two dozen other lakes, in adjoining cirques draining to French and Leland Creeks and over the ridge of Granite Mountain, draining to the Cle Elum River. Rude paths may be found to any big enough to support a trout. Some aren't, and that's a mercy.

Klonaqua Lakes and Granite Mountain

French Ridge

35 FRENCH RIDGE

Round trip to lookout site 12 miles
Hiking time 6 hours
High point 5800 feet
Elevation gain 3000 feet

Hikable July through September
One day or backpack
USGS Stevens Pass and
Chiwaukum Mountains

A large, green meadow, former site of a lookout tower, with commanding views up and down the Icicle valley and to distant peaks. For day trips the approach described here is better; overnighters wishing a loop might prefer to come via French Creek and the Backdoor Trail.

Drive the Icicle Creek road to the end, elevation 2900 feet, and hike the Icicle Creek trail 1½ miles to French Ridge trail No. 1564, 3100 feet (Hike 30). On the way, at 1¼ miles, pass French Creek–Backdoor Trail, an alternate entry for an overnight loop hike or the exit for a one-day loop (Hike 32).

From a gentle start the French Ridge trail progresses to serious switchbacking up the narrow crest of the tip of the ridge. In 3½ miles (from the road) the angle moderates a while, at 4½ miles steepens again. At 5½ miles the way emerges from woods into meadows, gaining a round green knoll, 6 miles, 5800 feet. Eat your kipper snacks and drink your lemonade and admire the panoramas the lookout used to scan for smoke.

By adding a full water carrier to the pack, a party could camp on the knoll and count stars.

The long-leggity may do the loop in a day, reducing the duration of thirst. Continue on the ridge trail from the knoll a scant 1½ miles to the Turquoise Lake junction, descend forest of the Backdoor Trail to the French Creek trail, and so on out to the Icicle trail and road, for a road-to-road loop of 14 miles.

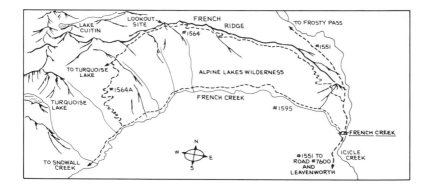

36 LAKE MARY

Round trip to Lake Mary 16 miles
Allow 2–3 days
High point 6200 feet
Elevation gain 3300 feet

Hikable mid-July through
October
USGS Chiwaukum Mountains

If the Enchantments are the granite classic of the Alpine Lakes Wilderness, Snowgrass Mountain is the supreme green. This is the place for dreamlike wanderings along tundra ridges and through lake basins and around corners to magic surprises. But there is a price to pay: a gang of dreamers, hordes of dreamers, wandering everywhere—many on horseback.

Drive the Icicle Creek road to the end, elevation 2900 feet, and hike the Icicle Creek trail 2 miles to Frosty Creek–Wildhorse trail No. 1592, 3000 feet (Hike 30).

Cross Icicle Creek on a bridge and start up. Soon cross Frosty Creek. There's a dry hill coming, with many a dusty switchback. But the worst is over at 6 miles, 4900 feet, when the way emerges from trees into the little basin of Packrat Camp. At 6¾ miles a short sidepath drops a bit to woodsy Lake Margaret, 5409 feet; camping is very limited. At 7½ miles the trail tops Frosty Pass, 5800 feet, and opens out into meadow-and-parkland that stretches in every direction as far as eye can see. Where to start?

An unsigned, unmaintained trail contours northwest from the pass to an excellent camp and continues sketchily onward—ultimately to Doelle Lakes (Hike 12). The Wildhorse trail sidehills north, giving off-trail (meadow) access to Grace Lakes (Hike 14).

Eventually one must proceed east from Frosty Pass on Icicle Ridge trail No. 1570, in ½ mile reaching the sidetrail dropping to Lake Mary, 6100 feet, the popular place for a basecamp, and a superb spot it is—if you can find a vacancy. If not, climb the garden-wall trail ¾ mile to Mary Pass, 6800 feet, and drop ½ mile to Upper Florence Lake, 6400 feet, with the most scenic—and most exposed—camps of all.

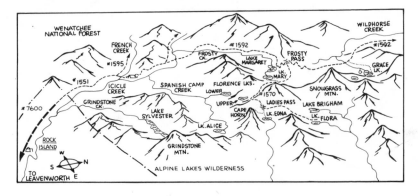

Mount Grindstone from Upper Florence Lake

Why stop? Just 1¼ flowery miles from Mary Pass is Ladies Pass, 6800 feet, above Lake Brigham and Lake Flora in headwaters of Chiwaukum Creek (Hike 17). In another mile, beyond the shoulder of 7300-foot Cape Horn, is Lake Edna, 6735 feet, a cold and rocky tarn (Hike 28). Spanish Camp Basin, below the trail to Ladies Pass, is well worth an afternoon; an old trail enters the basin from Upper Florence Lake. For high panoramas leave the trail at Mary Pass and strike up the way trail to the 7500-foot ridge of Snowgrass Mountain and views from Cashmere and Stuart to Monte Cristo and Glacier to Index and Baring. Or leave the trail between Lake Mary and Mary Pass and climb to a hidden basin and continue upward to an even higher ridge of Snowgrass. (The several summits of the 4-mile-long mountain, the highest 8000 feet, require climbing experience and equipment, but easy hiking takes a person high enough to feel on top of the world.)

To preserve vegetation, campers are asked to use established sites.

Icicle Creek road	Old:	2512
	New:	7600

37   LAKE LELAND

Round trip 23 miles	**Hikable mid-July through**
Allow 2–3 days	**September**
High point 4461 feet	**USGS Chiwaukum Mountains,**
Elevation gain 1600 feet	**Stevens Pass, The Cradle**

This is an unpretentious trip, the sort a hiker luxuriating in lonesomeness might describe as "an ill-favored thing, but mine own." The trail is muddy, brushy, crosses many creeks and windfalls, and scarcely sees a maintenance crew from one decade to the next. All the better for a person with whom the world is too much, late and soon, wasting his powers. Camps are pleasant, the views from subalpine Lake Leland very fine to cliffs of Granite and Trico Mountains, and a goat-nimble hiker can scramble around in steep heather and enjoy views from atop those cliffs.

Drive the Icicle Creek road to the end, elevation 2900 feet, and hike the Icicle Creek trail 6 miles to Leland Creek trail No. 1566, 3240 feet (Hike 30).

From the camp at the site of vanished Bark Cabin the trail crosses Icicle Creek on a large bridge to more camps. In a few hundred feet the path splits, Lorraine Ridge trail No. 1568 (Hike 38) going right. Go left ¼ mile to a crossing of Leland Creek, leaving the Icicle Creek valley for that of Leland Creek. At 8 miles (from the Icicle Creek road) is a small but comfy camp, 3400 feet, and another split in the trail, the right fork heading for Square Lake (Hike 39).

Go left and at 9¼ miles reach the end of the lower valley, wide and gentle, and enter the narrow and steep upper valley, the briskly climbing trail paralleling a cascading Leland Creek. At 10½ miles is a small camp and at 11½ miles are more camps at the lake, 4461 feet.

The lake sits in too deep a hole to be the best possible base for highland wanderings. However, boot-beaten paths round the lake to the left, giving views of French Ridge east, Trico Mountain south, and the long,

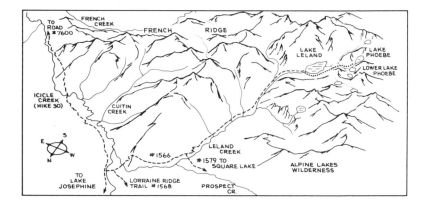

Trico Mountain from Lake Leland

many-peaked ridge of Granite Mountain southwest. In late summer the outlet stream may be crossed on a logjam to an abandoned and sketchy trail that climbs 1½ miles to the three Phoebe Lakes, the highest 5214 feet, at the very bottom of Trico's cliffs. Goat paths can be found winding up steep rockslides and heather parklands to Granite Mountain Potholes (Hike 74).

Icicle Creek valley from Lorraine Ridge trail

ICICLE CREEK
Alpine Lakes Wilderness

 LORRAINE RIDGE

Round trip to Lake Lorraine 20 miles
Allow 2–3 days
High point 5451 feet
Elevation gain 2700 feet in, 450 feet out

Hikable July through September
USGS Chiwaukum Mountains and Stevens Pass

Fill all available canteens and plod straight up a trail built by early fire lookouts who didn't wish to waste time getting to and from work. Sit on the ground by the site of their long-gone cabin, nibble your blue cheese and liver sausage, and gaze at peaks and ridges from Icicle Ridge to Stevens Pass and the topper, Glacier Peak. Then wander along the ridge, sniffing the flowers, and drop to a small lake with nice camps.

Drive the Icicle Creek road to the end, elevation 2900 feet, and hike the Icicle Creek and Leland Creek trails 6¼ miles to Lorraine Ridge trail No. 1568, 3200 feet (Hikes 30 and 37).

The hasty trail takes dead aim on the ridge crest along a steep rib; in ½ mile the rib becomes so ridiculously steep as to make flexing the ankles a problem, so a few switchbacks are thrown in. At the end of the sixth switchback, walk out left for a breather and views up Leland Creek and down Icicle Creek. At 2½ miles (from Icicle Creek) the twenty-first switchback and forest end at a rock buttress, the start of a final ½-mile ascent so busy with views that no excuse is needed for going slow.

Approaching the crest, the trail quits climbing and turns left to contour along a bench. Spot a faint old path heading uphill right, drop packs, and in ⅛ mile sit down at the site of the lookout, 5451 feet, a bit below the summit of Lake Lorraine Point. Get out the maps and spend some time reciting the names of the peaks you see, such as Bulls Tooth to the west, Cowboy Mountain north, Mac Peak southwest.

Returned to the packs, continue ½ mile along the trail, near and on the ridge crest, and descend 450 feet to small camps at Lake Lorraine, 5056 feet, 4 miles from the Icicle Creek trail, 10 from the Icicle Creek road.

The ridge path proceeds on the crest, faintly, beaten out by goat hooves, and circles above the lake to a viewpoint above Trapper Creek. The goats probably also have a route to Thunder Mountain Lakes, but that's their business.

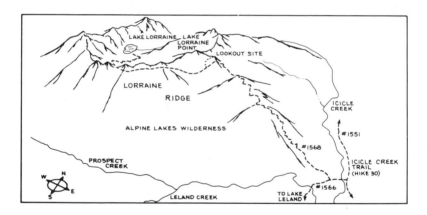

39   SQUARE LAKE

Round trip 23 miles
Allow 2–4 days
High point 5120 feet
Elevation gain 2220 feet

Hikable August through
   mid-October
USGS Chiwaukum Mountains and
   Stevens Pass

Many a hiker, ascending to the Cascade Crest from the west side of the mountains and finding himself just over the ridge from Square Lake, has considered scrambling over the splintered and cliffy granite ridge connecting Mac Peak and Thunder Mountain, having heard the lake and its companions are very pretty. Generally, however, off-trail explorers turn back, deciding to try again next time from the east side of the mountains, via trail—the easy way. Should they so persevere they will be rewarded by not only beauty but peace and pristinity—because there is no easy way. Stoicism will triumph over the ankle-deep mud and head-high brush and the barricades of logs to be crawled over and under. It takes something more, though, to manage the two fords of raging creeks. There's no such thing as a free lunch.

Drive the Icicle Creek road to the end, elevation 2900 feet, and hike the Icicle Creek and Leland Creek trails 8 miles to the Square Lake trail, 3400 feet (Hikes 30 and 37).

There is a bridge across Leland Creek, an old shaky thing not safe enough for horses but, as long as it lasts, good enough for feet. There is now a second crossing of the same creek. After a steep ¾-mile ascent into the valley of Prospect Creek there is a third, of this new creek. Now the worst is over: nothing left to fear but mud, brush, and windfalls. The

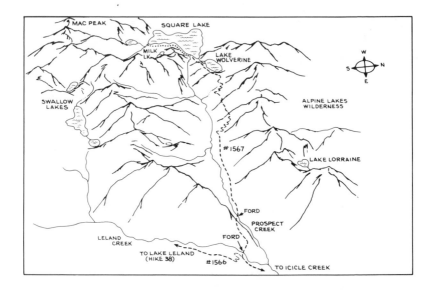

Square Lake

climb is moderate until a series of large avalanche swaths from Thunder Mountain, where the trail is faint and greenery-choked. Just before the first swath, 1¾ miles from Leland Creek, is a small camp. Shortly afterward switchbacks begin, starting in brush, continuing in forest.

At 3¼ miles from Leland Creek is the rocky cirque of Lake Wolverine, 5041 feet; no camps here, carry on. The way descends gently in the final ¼ mile to Square Lake, 4989 feet, 11½ miles from the Icicle Creek road. Follow the trail around the shore to the outlet, which was dammed in the remote pre-EIS past by Icicle Irrigation District to maintain the flow of Icicle Creek in times of drought. In low water the dam can be crossed with dry feet to an old guard cabin and a very limited camping area—an indication of the light use. If the way were quick and easy, hordes of fishermen and horsemen would have beaten out acres of bare ground.

By poking around a bit, explorers can find little Milk Lake and a second Square Lake, which also isn't square. Goats are suspected of ascending Mac Peak from here and possibly crossing the granite ramparts of Deception Lakes.

RED HILL

Round trip 9 miles
Hiking time 6 hours
High point 3840 feet
Elevation gain 2180 feet

Hikable May through
  mid-October
One day
USGS Monitor and Liberty
Motorcycle country

A long, rolling ridge whose dry-side-of-the-Cascades forests are broken by grassy "desert-alpine" meadows has views the length of the Wenatchee Mountains and, in late spring, weeks of flower color before the east-side sun shrivels the blossoms. The season of blooming marks the transition from the months when all this sector of the Cascades is racketing with snowmobiles to the months when it is racketing with motorcycles. Of the two routes to Red Hill, the one from Devils Gulch trail (Hike 42) is built as a motorcycle expressway and is very easy to follow, the track well-defined by wheels and the noise ear-splitting. The

Balsamroot alongside Red Hill trail

route described here has not been upgraded (degraded) to wheel standards and thus is relatively quiet, in the early part at least. However, once it enters the romper room, a hiker needs map and compass to navigate the maze of wheel tracks that interweave everywhere, running to and fro for the glee of the musclebutts.

Drive US 2 to Cashmere. If coming from the west, take the first exit to town; from the east, the second. Proceed to the stoplight in the town center and continue straight on Division Street, which bends right around a school to become Pioneer Street. At .4 mile from the light turn left on Mission Creek road for .5 mile to an unmarked intersection; turn right, cross Mission Creek, and take the first left back onto Mission Creek road and follow it 7.4 miles to an unmarked fork at pavement's end. Go right, at the next junction stay left, and in 1.8 miles from the pavement, 10.1 miles from the stoplight, come to a small unmarked campground, elevation 1660 feet.

Of the two trails from the campground take the left, Red Hill trail No. 1223, cross Sand Creek, the last water, on a bridge, and start the switchbacks.

At ¾ mile the way emerges from forest to dense brush of an old clearcut, crosses the loggers' skid road, and points straight up the hill for ½ mile of brush interlaced across the path. At 1¼ miles is a confusing intersection; go left up a steep pitch to where the trail suddenly is well-maintained, this being the motorcycle route from Devils Gulch.

On the ridge crest the forest opens and wheel paths branch in every direction. When in doubt take the less-steep choice, usually correct.

In 2½ miles little meadows begin breaking the forest and the views start. At 3½ miles pass a 3530-foot knoll and meander from meadow to meadow the final 1 mile to Red Hill; the 3840-foot summit lies several hundred feet west of the main trail.

Beyond, the trail resumes climbing, gaining 1000 feet in 1½ miles to meet the Tiptop–Mt. Lillian trail atop Tronsen Ridge (Hike 45) at 8 miles, 4790 feet.

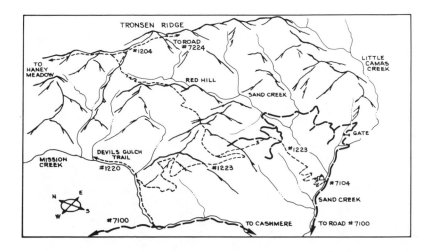

MISSION RIDGE

Round trip to viewpoint 4½ miles
Hiking time 3 hours
High point 3400 feet
Elevation gain 1650 feet

Hikable May through October
One day
USGS Cashmere, Liberty, Monitor
Motorcycle country

The subrange of the Cascades known as the Wenatchee Mountains lies
east of the crest in the sunshine country, the land of pine forests and several times the number of species of flowers at comparable elevations west
of the crest. The knife-edge of Mission Ridge samples the open forests and
brilliant little meadows, and the fine views as well: down sheer cliffs to
Devils Gulch and around its weird pinnacles, up to Mission Peak, west to
Tronsen Ridge and east to Horselake Mountains, and in the scenic
climaxes, the craggy-snowy Stuart Range to the west and, to the east, a
broad expanse of rolling hills lowering to the infinite flatness of the Columbia Plateau.

But ... all this lovely land has been "released" to wheels, one entire
geographical-ecological province in which quiet is a rare possibility,
where every valley and hill that can be motorcycled *is* motorcycled. The
trail here described was once well-graded with switchbacks for hikers
and horses; now it's a straight up-and-down wheel chute, becoming a
trench. By coming in midweek in late spring, when snowfields linger, a
hiker may be permitted to enjoy the flowers and views in peace, but for
months at a time no rational hiker or horse rider, only motorcyclists,
venture to this blighted garden.

Drive Mission Creek road to the fork at pavement's end (Hike 40). Go
left 2.7 miles to a turnoff. In 1984 the trailhead sign was missing but the
post was there, elevation 1750 feet.

The trail begins on a bridge over East Mission Creek to a fork. Devils
Gulch trail No. 1220 goes right (Hike 42). Go left on Mission Ridge trail
No. 1201 and start climbing. After the first switchback the way passes the
first rocky pinnacle to the opening out of vistas. The ascent is mainly in
the shade of pine trees, yet warm enough by a summer noon. Beyond the
rocky first mile the ridge broadens and the forest floor becomes grassy to

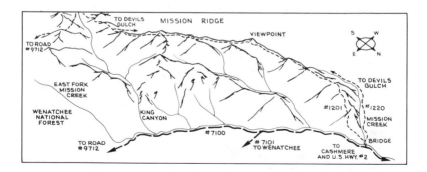

Mission Ridge

an old skid road at 2 miles. In another ¼ mile the ridge changes character again, reverting to rockiness. The lupine is especially lovely late June to mid-July; in a warm afternoon the perfume may put you to sleep the way it did the lotus-eaters seen by Odysseus.

At 2¼ miles the trail crests a small knoll. Go right on a rough footpath to a jutting rib, a superb viewpoint and a good spot to sit and drink your Gookinaid and eat your bagels and cream cheese.

From this knoll the trail takes a deep dip before climbing the next. At 6 miles it passes a group of large rock pinnacles where a tree 10 feet in diameter grows from naked rock. At 7½ miles is the high point of the route, 4900 feet, followed by a steep drop to meet the Devils Gulch trail (a loop!) at 8 miles, 4420 feet. From the junction the trail proceeds 2 more miles to the Liberty–Beehive road, a popular trip for motorcycles, bah, humbug.

Mission Creek road   Old: 2204
                      New: 7100

DEVILS GULCH

Round trip to last water 15 miles
Hiking time 7 hours
High point 3500 feet
Elevation gain 1750 feet
Hikable May through October
One day or backpack
USGS Cashmere, Liberty, Monitor
Motorcycle country

Mission Ridge loop trip 17 miles
Hiking time 10 hours
High point 4800 feet
Elevation gain 3050 feet
Hikable June through October

Travelers of olden days were reminded of the Devil by the narrow slot of the valley and the sheer cliffs of its steep walls, the unearthly pinnacles, and the scorching sun of summer. Hikers of today are reminded of Hell as they listen to motorcycles whining and snarling their paean to the Lord of the Flies. However, the good Creation cannot be abandoned to evil. By visiting in late spring or early summer, especially in the middle of the week, a hiker can savor the beauty of the flowers and enjoy the handiwork of the Devil (who in the Manichean heresy is said to be the Creator), so benign by comparison with His human imps.

Drive Mission Creek road beyond pavement's end 2.7 miles to the trailhead, elevation 1750 feet (Hike 41).

Cross East Mission Creek on a plank bridge to a fork. Mission Ridge trail No. 1201 goes left (Hike 41); go right on Devils Gulch trail No. 1220 and cross Mission Creek.

The trail is maintained (with your money) to motorcycle standards and has been rebuilt to let them razz as fast as possible, so look sharp and at blind corners honk your horn. After a single switchback the path begins a long traverse across a slope of rockslides and sheer cliffs interspersed with bands of forest. Note the abundance of animal signs and game traces. At ½ mile pass a sidetrail up Red Hill, a popular motocross area (Hike 40). Stump Camp, 2¼ miles, 2240 feet, is the first of three maintained campgrounds, should you take your chances on getting any sleep hereabouts, where machines roar by day and beer drinkers by night.

In ¼ mile the trail crosses Mission Creek on a bridge built for wheels

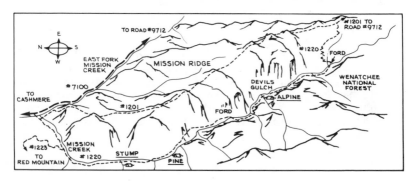

Devils Gulch trail

and makes a quick climb from forest back to the steep and open slopes of the gulch, colored in early July by wild roses. At 3 miles, 2360 feet, is Pine Camp; an old bridge serves as a large picnic table, a distinctive touch.

The next crossing of Mission Creek, 4½ miles, lacked a bridge in 1984; the high water of spring isn't too daunting to ford but does discourage many motorcyclists, who prefer mud wallows for fun. Beside a small tributary to Mission Creek is Alpine Camp, 6 miles, 3000 feet.

The path contours hillsides to the final and also bridgeless crossing of Mission Creek, 7½ miles, 3500 feet, a good turnaround for hikers not wishing to loop on over Mission Ridge and, for those who do, the last place to find water.

Switchbacks ascend 1½ miles to the crest of Mission Ridge and an intersection with Mission Ridge trail, 4420 feet. To complete the loop turn left (Hike 41).

Mission Creek road   Old: 2204
                                           New: 7100

43   INGALLS CREEK

Round trip to Falls Creek Camp 12 miles
Hiking time 6 hours
High point 3200 feet
Elevation gain 1200 feet
Hikable late May through October
One day or backpack
USGS Liberty and Mt. Stuart

Round trip to Stuart Pass 32 miles
Allow 3–5 days
High point 6400 feet
Elevation gain 4400 feet
Hikable July through September

The longest wilderness valley remaining in the Cascades outside the far north, 16 miles of trail climbing from low forest to high meadows passing constantly changing views of the spectacular Stuart Range.

Hike this trail the first week of June when the first 5 miles are lined with trillium, gold-colored paintbrush, and a few calypso orchids thrown in. If you're too early for trillium, there will be glacier lilies. If you're too late for trillium, there will be queen's cup.

Drive US 97 north from Swauk (Blewett) Pass 12.5 miles and turn left on Ingalls Creek road about 1 mile to the road-end and trailhead, elevation 1953 feet.

The trail ascends steadily but gently, alternating between groves of trees and patches of avalanche brush, mostly in sight and always in sound of roaring Ingalls Creek, with tantalizing glimpses of the rocky

Ingalls Creek near Falls Creek

Trilliums

summits of the Stuart Range, and later, looks to fantastic spires.

In early June hikers usually will encounter snow patches from 4 miles or so and difficult going beyond the vicinity of Falls Creek, 6 miles, 3200 feet. The lovely Falls Creek Camp is reached by a sidetrail across Ingalls Creek, which is much too deep and swift to ford while meltwater is rushing. In any season this point makes a good turnaround for day trippers.

The way continues upward along the almost-straight fault-line valley (granite on one side, sediments and metamorphics on the other), the forest becoming subalpine and open, the views growing. Tributary creeks are crossed often; pleasant camps are frequent.

From Porcupine Creek, about 10 miles, 4100 feet, the path steepens a bit and sidehills above Ingalls Creek, the timber increasingly broken by meadows. Now the cliffs and buttresses of 9415-foot Mt. Stuart, second-highest nonvolcanic peak in the state, dominate the scene.

At about 13½ miles, 4800 feet, the trail nears Ingalls Creek and commences a rather earnest ascent, climbing parkland and flowers and talus to Stuart Pass, 16 miles, 6400 feet. On the far side the tread descends Jack Creek to Chatter Creek Forest Station on Icicle Creek.

All along the upper valley the open country invites wanderings on side trails, such as Longs Pass (Hike 58). From a camp in the delightful basin under Stuart Pass one can spend days exploring—begin by contouring from the pass to 6463-foot Ingalls Lake (Hike 57).

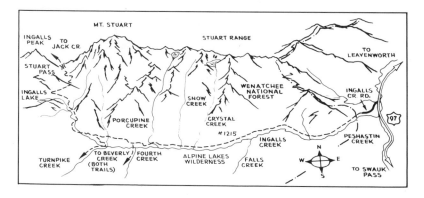

44 MOUNT LILLIAN LOOPS

Short loop trip 7 miles
Hiking time 4 hours
High point 6000 feet
Elevation gain 400 feet
Hikable late June through
    September

One day or backpack
USGS Liberty
Motorcycle country

Long loop trip 11¼ miles
Hiking time 6 hours
Elevation gain 800 feet

A short loop hike traverses varied terrain of forest and meadow and ever-changing scenery of the Wenatchee Mountains. A longer loop gives the same but lots more of it, the more exciting for secluded meadows, striking viewpoints, and numerous sidetrails to explore.

Drive US 97 to Swauk Pass and turn south on road No. 9716, following "Table Mountain" signs. In 3.8 miles go left on road No. 9712 another 4.9 miles to Haney Meadow. To do the long loop, park at the campground, elevation 5502 feet. For the short loop park .2 mile farther along on the Old Ellensburg Trail, at 5480 feet.

Short loop: Hike road No. 9712 for ¾ mile from the Old Ellensburg Trail to Tiptop–Mt. Lillian trail No. 1204 (Hike 45) and follow it ¼ mile up the valley to an unmarked junction. Go right on a heavily traveled (wheels and all) trail heading rapidly uphill. At 1¾ miles pass a remarkable viewpoint down cliffs to Devils Gulch, 3000 feet below, and out northeast to a sparkle of the Columbia River.

Ascend a knoll and plunge past rocky pinnacles, the trail churned by horses and rutted by wheels, at 2½ miles emerging abruptly on road No. 9712. Walk the road east 1000 feet to Howard Creek trail No. 1372 and descend it through meadows and forest, beside the rippling creek, 1¾ miles to Old Ellensburg Trail No. 1373 and a small camp. Take the Old Ellensburg Trail 2 miles back to Haney Meadow to close the loop.

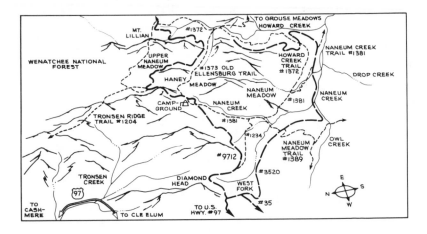

Overlooking Devils Gulch from a shoulder of Mount Lillian

Long loop: Continue down Howard Creek a scant ¼ mile to a junction where Old Ellensburg Trail goes left to Grouse Meadow; go right on Howard Creek trail, which turns sharply right and starts climbing. Scenery soon opens from a grassy ridge; across the deep gorge of Howard Creek can be seen a fine display of columnar basalt.

At 5 miles from Haney Meadow the trail enters a series of clearcuts. Cross a skid road and continue straight, winding around logs and stumps, following a dry streambed, and contouring the edge of a clearcut. Beware of cows giving you the evil eye, a warning to find some other spot to sit and chew your cud.

Howard Creek joins Naneum Creek and the trail rounds the south corner of the loop, crossing another road, passing numerous vistas over the two creeks and the flat top of Table Mountain to the west. At 8¼ miles from Haney Meadow Howard Creek trail ends at Naneum Creek trail No. 1381, 5200 feet.

Continue straight on this new name, by several possible camps, gently ascending small meadows. At 9 miles the way suddenly drops in several switchbacks to Naneum Meadow and a junction with Naneum Meadow trail No. 1389, 5200 feet.

Cross the meadow, passing the stock gate, circling cliffs of columnar basalt, crossing a muddy creek. At 9¼ miles the trail passes another stock gate at the upper end of the meadow; here is Naneum Camp, a comfortable spot.

Naneum Rim trail branches left; continue straight along Naneum Creek to road No. 9712, reached at 11 miles from the loop start. Cross the road and a small rib to return to Haney Meadow Campground, 11¼ miles.

Sandstone cliff on Tronsen Ridge

SWAUK CREEK
Unprotected area

 TRONSEN RIDGE

Round trip to Red Hill trail 8 miles
Hiking time 5 hours
High point 5840 feet
Elevation gain 240 feet in, 970 feet
  out

Hikable mid-June through
  September
One day
USGS Liberty
Motorcycle country

A classic ridge walk over rolling hills of the Wenatchee Mountains gives splendid views west to snowy peaks of the Cascades and east to heat-shimmering plains of Columbia River country. An enjoyable hike can be had by going little more than a mile from the start; the ambitious can explore another 5 miles beyond the suggested turnaround—chosen because Mt. Adams is visible, a satisfying way to cap the climax.

Drive to Haney Meadow (Hike 44) and .9 mile beyond to Tiptop–Mt. Lillian trail No. 1204 in Upper Naneum Meadow, elevation 5623 feet. (Don't be confused by the Tronsen Meadow trail—it leads downhill only.)

The first ¼ mile, walk either the trail on the left side of little Naneum Creek or the road on the right side, the two joining just before Mt. Lillian trail splits off to the right; stay left on the road. Near the end of the first mile it tops a grassy knoll and bends left. Here the ridge trail leaves the road and drops right, into forest; for a terrific view of the Stuart Range, Mt. Rainier, and a whole lot else, stay on the road to the end on a rocky point, then follow a motorcycle rut steeply down to the trail.

The way rolls along the crest of Tronsen Ridge, climbing in short spurts to summits and falling back down to saddles. Motorcycle fun-tracks shortcut and crisscross; choose the gentlest angle up or down to stay on the real trail.

At about 3 miles US 97 comes in view when the path dips to the west side of the ridge to traverse beneath picturesque sandstone spires, a rock climber's delight. At 3¾ miles pass a wheel shortcut to Red Hill trail No. 1223 (Hike 40) and in ¼ mile more reach the official junction. See Mt. Adams, kill off the sardines and the root beer, and return.

Or, continue to road No. 7224 at 7 miles, the abandoned West Sand Creek trail at 8 miles, and the end of the ridge trail at Ruby Creek in 9 miles. Study the map and invent loops.

Table Mountain road	Old:	2107	Tronsen Ridge road	Old:	2209
	New:	9716		New:	7224
Haney Meadow road	Old:	2100			
	New:	9712			

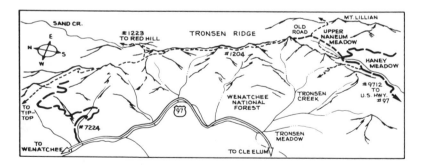

46 BLEWETT RIDGE

Round trip to Miller Peak 10½ miles	**Hikable July through mid-October**
Hiking time 7 hours	**One day**
High point 6400 feet	**USGS Liberty**
Elevation gain 1700 feet plus ups and downs	**Motorcycle country**

Airy meadows of the narrow crest look out to the Wenatchee Mountains, pure motorcycle country, and high ice and rock of the Stuart Range, pure wilderness. Blewett Ridge is the nearest thing to a wilderness experience possible in a locality dissected by public and private logging operations, largely because though the trail has been partly rebuilt—on National Forest sections only—to let motorcycles run fast and loose, the starting point is so obscure it rarely receives any use whatsoever.

Part of the County Line trail (Hike 52), the Blewett Ridge trail starts at Blewett Pass. The early stretch, however, is very brushy and hard to follow, so a beginning a mile or so along the old route is described here. Getting to it is no cinch because the logging roads are mostly private and unmaintained and have no numbers or signs. Your car may suggest that you walk all or some of the road distance from Blewett Pass, elevation 4064.

Drive US 97 north 3.2 miles from Mineral Spring Resort or 4.8 miles west from Swauk Pass and take the Old Blewett Road 3.8 miles to Blewett Pass. At the summit turn left, steeply uphill, on a very poor private road. In .2 mile turn left at the first junction and at .5 mile left again, sidehilling downward. At the bottom take a very hard left. In 2000 feet go right .7 mile, crossing the crest of Blewett Ridge and dropping. At the bottom look left to spot the unmarked trailhead, elevation 4700 feet.

The trail climbs steadily the first mile to gain the 5440-foot summit of the ridge's first attainment of mile-high elevation. Near the top the path is cut by a logging road; head straight up from the last recognizable por-

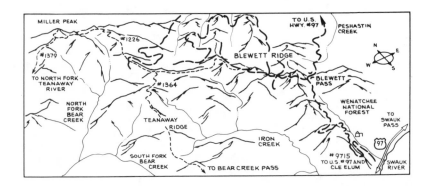

County Line Trail near Miller Peak

tion of trail to find it again.

The big views begin as the route waltzes along the crest from summit to summit, switching from side to side. A steep descent of woods and ascent of a field of grass lead to Teanaway Ridge trail No. 1364 (Hike 47). Proceed west, dropping to a clearcut in a saddle and beginning the climb of open meadows to Miller Peak.

At 4 miles the trail quits the ridge for a long contour around Miller Peak to new views of Navaho Peak and Mt. Stuart. At 5 miles, 5600 feet, join the Miller Peak trail (Hike 49) for the final ¼-mile push to the summit, 6000 feet, which might logically be considered the terminus of Blewett Ridge, though the divide goes on to more peaks.

Mount Stuart and Miller Peak from Teanaway Ridge

SWAUK CREEK
Unprotected area

 **IRON CREEK–
TEANAWAY RIDGE**

**Round trip to 5489-foot knoll 6
  miles**
Hiking time 4 hours
High point 5489 feet
Elevation gain 1900 feet

**Hikable mid-June through
  mid-October**
One day
USGS Liberty
Motorcycle country

A relatively short climb (but dry; carry loaded canteens) brings rich dividends of meadows and views—nearby to the Stuart Range, far away to Rainier. Once the ridge is attained the highline rambling can go for miles, in several directions. Sorry to say—as must be done so often in the east-slope Cascades—it's motorcycle country, the trails rebuilt (*not* "improved") for speedy wheeling. Until this madness is halted the hike is best done midweek, when there is some chance of being able to hear bird songs and bumblebee buzzes.

Drive US 97 north 2.3 miles from Mineral Spring Resort or 5.7 miles west from Swauk Pass and make a sharp turn west off the highway and immediately north onto Iron Creek road No. 9714. In 3.6 miles are the road-end and Iron Creek–Bear Creek trail No. 1351, elevation 3600 feet.

The trail sets out steeply up the barren, rubbly slopes characteristic of this area—in late spring through the anomalous exuberance of flowers also characteristic. At 1 mile attain Iron Creek–Bear Creek Pass, 4480 feet, and a four-way stop. The straight-ahead trail drops 3½ miles down Bear Creek to road No. 9738. Teanaway Ridge trail No. 1364 goes left 3½ up-and-down miles to road No. (9702)120. Turn right on a new section of the latter trail, the route to the high country.

The way ascends the narrow and rocky crest of the ridge, then traverses with long switchbacks up an ancient burn, views expanding by the step, at 3 miles from the road topping out on a 5489-foot knoll, a great place to get out the maps and the granola bars and the chocolate-chip cookies. Miller Peak is only 1½ air miles distant, the snow-patched and granite-walled crags of the Stuart Range beyond; Stuart is seen from here as a sharp-cleavered triangular peak notably higher than its neighbors. Tronsen Ridge is east. South looms the big white mound of Mt. Rainier.

For the information of ridgerunners, from here the trail drops 300 feet and at 4 miles climbs to the Blewett Ridge segment of County Line trail No. 1226, which leads in either direction through flowers and views (Hike 46).

Iron Creek road	Old:	2212	Bear Creek road	Old:	2226
	New:	9714		New:	9738
Blue Creek road	Old:	2106			
	New:	(9702)120			

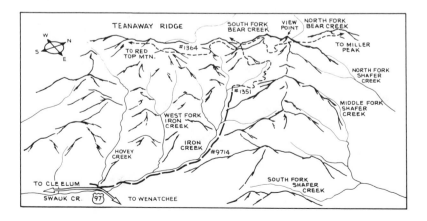

48 NAVAHO PASS

Round trip 11 miles
Hiking time 5 hours
High point 6000 feet
Elevation gain 2900 feet

Hikable mid-June through
  September
One day or backpack
USGS Mt. Stuart
Motorcycle country

Hike close along a babbling-burbling stream, passing many nice camps, climbing quite steeply and clambering over a few logs (the better to discourage the wheel-freaks), up through brilliant dry-site gardens to a high pass with stupendous views across Ingalls Creek to the Stuart Range.

Drive Highway 970 north 5 miles from Interstate 90 and turn west on Teanaway River road. Follow "North Fork Teanaway" signs 13.5 miles to a major junction at 29 Pines Campground. Go right 1.3 miles on road No. 9737, then right on Stafford Creek road No. 9738, in 2.5 miles crossing Stafford Creek to Stafford Creek–Cascade Creek trail No. 1359, elevation 3100 feet.

The trail starts on an old jeep track, quickly narrows to the real thing, and climbs steadily but rarely steeply, sometimes beside the creek and other times a stone's throw above. The first 2 miles are through tall pine, hemlock, and silver fir. These thin out, yielding to the little dry-and-stony meadows typical of the area, the plants sparse but in early summer blooming in all colors of the rainbow.

At 4 miles, 5100 feet, is a junction with Standup Creek trail No. 1369. Confusingly, the trail signs imply that Stafford Creek trail becomes Standup Creek trail. Whatever, go right, following the sign pointing to "Negro Creek trail 1 mile"; be prepared for 1½ or 2 miles. The way makes a long switchback with downvalley views, then climbs in short switchbacks to a pass just west of Navaho Peak and thus here dubbed "Navaho Pass," 5½ miles, 6000 feet.

The pass is on the boundary of the Alpine Lakes Wilderness, which en-

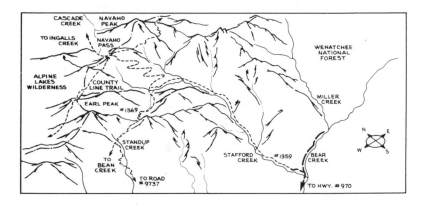

Mount Stuart Range from Navaho Pass

compasses the deep gulf of Ingalls Creek beneath and the high-leaping wall of the Stuart Range beyond. Mt. Stuart itself is cut off from view, but Little Annapurna and 8364-foot McClellan Peak are most acceptable stand-ins.

At the pass is a four-way intersection. Cascade Creek trail drops 5 miles to Ingalls Creek. To the east, the slopes of 7223-foot Navaho Peak are traversed by Negro Creek trail. (*Note:* The original name, as late as the 1960s used on government maps, was the racial epithet used by the miners, but long since abandoned by decent people. The government very properly amended its maps but in so doing substituted a term once considered polite but now felt by most Americans of African descent to be as demeaning as the epithet.) To the west the County Line trail, less a real trail (Hike 52) than a figment of the imagination, follows the ridge crest a ways, contours around a high point, and drops to Hardscrabble Creek basin.

North Fork Teanaway road	Old:	232
	New:	9737
Stafford Creek road	Old:	2226
	New:	9738

123

49 MILLER PEAK

Round trip 9 miles
Hiking time 5 hours
High point 6400 feet
Elevation gain 3200 feet

Hikable July through September
One day
USGS Mt. Stuart and Liberty
Motorcycle country

A glorious viewpoint of the dark massif of the Stuart Range, the arid-brown Wenatchee Range overlooking Swauk and Blewett Passes, the huge whiteness of Mt. Rainier and Mt. Adams, and considerable greenery amid the rocks of nearby Navaho Peak, Three Brothers, and Iron Mountain.

Drive Stafford Creek road (Hike 48) 3.5 miles to the end at the confluence of Miller and Bear Creeks and the parking lot for their trails, elevation 3200 feet.

Miller Creek boasts another of the motorcycle expressways that infest the area, but in midweek when the wheels are away the hikers can play, far more quietly. The trail starts on the west side of the creek but soon switches to the east. On this crossing and the several that follow, logjams and boulders must serve as footbridges.

A gentle ascent 2 miles along the creek brings the valley end. Gaze far above to green meadows and think what a haul the getting there must be. It is. Switchbacks handsomely graded for wheels climb and climb, at 3½ miles, 5200 feet, attaining a saddle in the ridge jutting from Miller Peak between Miller and Bear Creek valleys. Here are the first broad views.

The way traverses the west side of the ridge over steep, green meadows to meet the County Line trail (Hikes 52 and 46) at 4 miles; the camp at the junction has no water after the snows melt. A final ¼ mile switchbacks to a saddle 300 feet below the summit, the stopping place of trail and motorcycles. A meager bootpath completes the ascent of the rock

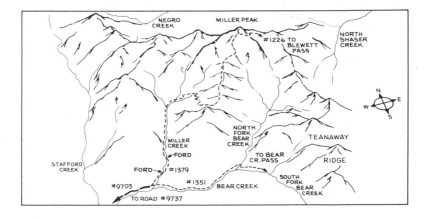

Balsamroot

summit, cliffs on three sides, too airy for most folks to enjoy on a foggy day, and some in sunshine. From the peak or the trail's end, views will keep your head swinging from side to side almost too fast for your carrot sticks and celery stalks to find your mouth.

To the south along Blewett Ridge (Hike 46) the County Line trail is groomed for motorcycles, suggesting to a hiker equipped with ice ax the advantages of visiting in June, when snowfields keep the peace. For a loop, follow this trail to the Iron Creek–Bear Creek trail, the return to the parking lot; 12¾ miles, a nice day. Experienced wildland navigators can have good sport trying to follow the County Line Trail north; not maintained and through the meadows never even built, the route is notably uncrowded.

North Fork Teanaway road	Old:	232
	New:	9737
Stafford Creek road	Old:	2226
	New:	9738

50   BEAN CREEK BASIN

Round trip to upper basin 4 miles
Hiking time 3 hours
High point 5600 feet
Elevation gain 1700 feet

Hikable mid-June through
  mid-October
One day
USGS Mt. Stuart
Motorcycle country

What's your pleasure? Views to Mt. Stuart and the Columbia Plateau?
These are to be had by climbing above Bean Creek Basin to the ridge
tops. Or are you content with wet meadows where the monkeyflower and
willow herb bloom and dry meadows of the buckwheat and skyrocket
gilia? If so, the basin floor is your game.

From Stafford Creek junction (Hike 48) drive North Fork Teanaway
road No. 9737 1.6 miles to Beverly Creek, 16.5 miles from Highway 970.
Just before crossing the creek, turn right 1.1 miles on Beverly Creek road
No. (9737)112 to the end, elevation 3600 feet.

Set out on Beverly–Turnpike trail No. 1391, the first ½ mile on old logging road through clearcuts. Just before the unbridged crossing of Bean
Creek go off right on Bean Creek trail No. 1391A, which soon leaves logged land for forest and begins a relentless, steep ascent of the valley. At
¼ mile cross Bean Creek—easily on boulders in late summer; with wet
feet and hips while the snowmelt is rushing, this unfortunately coincid-
ing with the time of richest blooming.

Alternating between bright mountain gardens and cool mountain
forests, the way comes to the lower basin and a split in the trail at 1½
miles, 5100 feet. Here you must choose your pleasure.

For sensational views, turn right on Bean Creek trail and climb 1½
miles to a 6150-foot shoulder southwest of Earl Peak and continue ½
mile, joining the Standup Creek trail, to a 5888-foot saddle on the southeast ridge of Earl. This section of trail is rarely used and poorly defined,

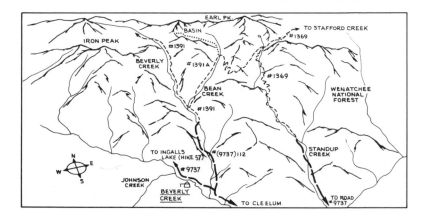

Bean Creek Basin

especially in meadows; the occasional cairn helps solve puzzlements.

From the 5100-foot junction in Bean Creek valley a trail forges resolutely forward a couple of hundred feet and abruptly dies. Continue along faint bootpaths on either side of the creek ½ mile to lush meadows of the upper basin, 5600 feet.

For flowers of the dry meadows proceed up the basin as it bends west, leaving trees behind. For views to top off the trip climb to the ridge at 6400 feet, and from the boundary of the Alpine Lakes Wilderness look the Stuart Range right in the face, as well as Earl and Iron Peaks and Beverly and Ingalls Creeks.

Beverly Creek road   Old: 232A
                        New: (9737)112

51 BEVERLY–TURNPIKE

**Round trip to Ingalls Creek 15
  miles
Allow 2 days
High point 5800 feet
Elevation gain 2200 feet in, 1000
  feet out**

**Hikable mid-July through
  mid-October
USGS Mt. Stuart**

Cross a high pass from the Teanaway River valley to Ingalls Creek.
Climb through open forests, flower fields, rock gardens, and views, including 9415-foot Mt. Stuart, second-highest non-volcanic mountain in
the state. In proper season the flowers begin at the trailhead and never
quit, climaxing in the weird, desertlike serpentine barrens for which the
area is famed among botanists. A stream crossing near the start can give
trouble in the high water of early summer.

Drive to the end of Beverly Creek road, elevation 3600 feet (Hike 50).

Trail No. 1391 starts steeply up a clearcut, quickly passing a junction
with the Bean Creek trail (Hike 50) and then facing the high-water challenge, the crossing of Bean Creek. The trail sidehills high above Beverly
Creek on a rocky hillside, brilliant at the right time with the yellow of
buckwheat and the scarlet of gilia, and at 2½ miles meets Fourth Creek
trail, a possible alternate return. Beverly Creek is crossed and switchbacks climb to 5800-foot Beverly–Turnpike Pass, 3½ miles.

The north side of the pass is thick-forested, so if one is not going on, for
views of Stuart climb the hill to the left (west) of the pass. But the really
terrific sidetrip from here is on the Iron Peak trail (Hike 55), hit just before the pass, leading up to the serpentine barrens and a superb ridge-
crest stroll in crazy rocks and violent flowers and big views down to and
across the Teanaway River.

From the pass the trail drops through woods, then switchbacks steeply
down a barren avalanche slope to the valley bottom and a pleasant forest
walk along Turnpike Creek. At 6 miles, by a nice campsite, is a crossing
of the creek (again, possibly difficult). The way then climbs a bit and
drops to a crossing of Ingalls Creek—unless a log (scarce) can be found,

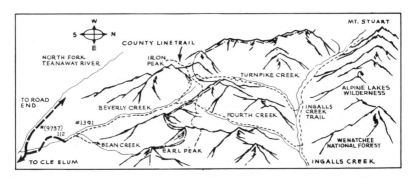

this is impossible at high water. On the far side is the Ingalls Creek trail (Hike 43). For a loop trip, follow the Ingalls Creek trail downstream 1½ miles to the junction with Fourth Creek trail, recross Ingalls Creek, and follow Fourth Creek up to its source, cross the ridge, and rejoin the Beverly–Turnpike trail.

Mount Stuart from Beverly–Turnpike Pass

Mount Stuart from County Line Trail

NORTH FORK TEANAWAY RIVER
Partially in Alpine Lakes Wilderness

52   COUNTY LINE TRAIL

One-way trip from Highway 970 to
  Teanaway River road about 24
  miles
Allow 3–4 days
High point 6300 feet
Elevation gain 3500 feet

Hikable mid-June through
  October
USGS Mt. Stuart and Liberty

The Wenatchee Mountain crest, boundary of two counties, offers two sets of spectacular views: from the Chelan County side, to rugged peaks of the Stuart Range; from the Kittitas County side, to foothills and farmlands. Presently the trip offers solitude, at a price—about half the trail, built in the 1920s for patrol work and abandoned prior to World War II, has totally vanished and most of the rest is sketchy. This part, therefore, is not your usual trail walk but rather a route to be attempted only with the aid of Forest Service and USGS maps. It's not tough for experienced wilderness navigators to follow in clear weather, but a party engulfed in clouds had best beat a quick retreat.

That's the *good* news. The bad news is that the Forest Service, using your tax funds, has mostly rebuilt the eastern section as far as Miller Peak as a motorcycle raceway. When the wheels ultimately are excluded (they must and will be) and the County Line trail is rebuilt the entire distance, it will form part of a splendid long journey from Blewett Pass to Stevens Pass. Keep the faith.

The eastern end of the County Line trail extends from Blewett Pass to Miller Peak (Hike 46). Tread effectively ends at the Miller Peak trail (Hike 49), 8 miles from Blewett Pass.

Scramble over the peak and follow ups and downs of the ridge crest toward Navaho Peak, sometimes on surviving bits of trail. At approximately 10 miles from Blewett Pass, on slopes of Navaho Peak, intersect Fall Creek trail and follow it westward a short mile to a saddle under Earl Peak and an intersection with trails from Stafford and Cascade Creeks.

For the next 3 airy miles the trail is plainer on maps than on the ground, but even where tread is utterly gone the walking is not all that difficult. At the intersection with Fourth Creek trail the County Line Trail is maintained ½ mile to the intersection with Beverly–Turnpike trail (Hike 51).

Descend the Beverly Creek trail a short bit and find Iron Peak trail (Hike 55), the abandoned route reopened in 1977 by the Youth Conservation Corps, climbing over a saddle and dropping 4 miles to the Teanaway River road.

Walk the road upvalley 1½ miles to the end and take the trail up Esmerelda Basin (Hike 56) to Fortune Creek Pass—or near. At ¼ mile short of the pass, at a little creek, the old trail route turns up right into a small basin and climbs to a divide on the ridge of Ingalls Peak. Drop to tiny Lake Ann, at the foot of the peak's walls, and follow an old sheep trail to Van Epps Pass, thence go via North Fork Fortune Creek to Scatter Creek trail, which descends to the Cle Elum River road (Hike 71).

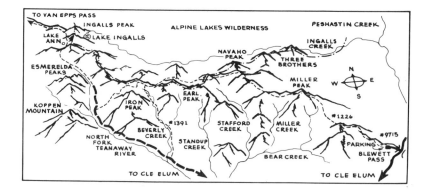

53   MEDRA PASS

Round trip 8 miles
Hiking time 5 hours
High point 5440 feet
Elevation gain 2340 feet

Hikable July through
   mid-October
One day
USGS Mt. Stuart

Follow a pretty creek through the forest for awhile, then climb rocky and flowery slopes awhile, then sit awhile at Medra Pass and look one way to Mt. Stuart and the other to Mt. Rainier and all around to valleys and ridges of Teanaway country.

From Stafford Creek junction (Hike 48) drive North Fork Teanaway River road 2.8 miles to Beverly Campground, 17.6 miles from Highway 970. Continue past the official camp area to an unofficial camp area. Park here or in a two-car space at the trailhead (unsigned in 1984), elevation 3100 feet.

Cross the North Fork Teanaway River on a sturdy horse bridge and wind along narrow Johnson Creek valley ¾ mile to a split in the trail. Trail No. 1383A goes left up South Fork Johnson Creek and over a wooded, 4500-foot ridge to Jungle Creek. Go right on trail No. 1383 up North Fork Johnson Creek, the forest broken by fields of brush. The path switches from the east side of the creek to the west, recrosses, and repeats the flip-flop in less than ½ mile; early-season hikers might keep drier feet by staying on the east side.

At 2¼ miles a switchback signals the end of water and a change in strategy. The way climbs the valley wall, leaving woods for opens, at 3½ miles attaining the top of the ridge. Views include the North Fork Teanaway valley below and, beyond, Mt. Stuart and the needle-crested Stuart Range. To these at Medra Pass, 4 miles, 5440 feet, are added the Middle Fork Teanaway valley and, seeming just over the next ridge, the gleaming slopes of Mt. Rainier.

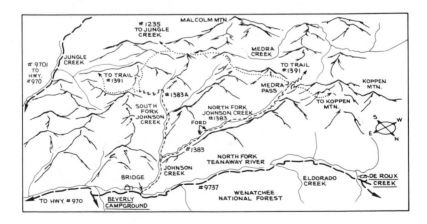

Mount Rainier from Medra Pass

The trail, very faint now, continues 2¼ miles down Medra Creek to the Middle Fork trail. However, if more exercise than the pass is wanted, the best views are north and south along the ridge crest. North 2 miles is Koppen Mountain (Hike 54). South the path wanders the tops 4 miles to join trail No. 1383A, a loop return to where you came from, if you are lucky.

54 KOPPEN MOUNTAIN

Round trip 7 miles
Hiking time 4 hours
High point 6031 feet
Elevation gain 2331 feet

Hikable July through September
One day
USGS Mt. Stuart
Motorcycle country

Look west over the Middle Fork Teanaway valley to meadowy ridges where Jolly Mountain overshadows companions, then turn around and take a single step east (the summit of Koppen Mountain is not large) and gaze over the North Fork Teanaway valley to the rock massif of Mt. Stuart and lesser foreground peaks, Iron and Esmerelda.

Drive North Fork Teanaway River road (Hike 48) 8.6 miles from Stafford Creek junction, 22.1 miles from Highway 970. Just beyond Eldorado Creek go off left on a bumpy road (unmarked in 1984) .3 mile to little De Roux Camp, elevation 3700 feet.

At the far end of the campground the unsigned Boulder–De Roux trail, pounded to powdery sand by hooves, heads up the valley, in some 1000 feet crosses the North Fork Teanaway on a bridge, and turns west, ascending a spectacular gorge of De Roux Creek. In a scant mile the way crosses the creek and quickly splits, at 4100 feet. The Boulder–De Roux trail climbs right, to Gallagher Head Lake and points beyond (Hike 56). Go left on Middle Fork Teanaway spur trail No. 1392A, ascending forest, then meadows, to the ridge top, 5100 feet, 1½ miles from the split. Turn left on the unmarked Koppen Mountain trail built in the 1930s when the mountain was an observation point for fire patrols. Today the trail is rough and poorly defined through green meadows and bare scree of bluish green serpentine.

Views to the left of you, views to the right of you. Those of Mt. Stuart framed by twisted old snags are breath-taking. At 3½ miles from the road a final push reaches the summit of Koppen Mountain, 6031 feet.

It's been such a relaxing morning that after all the rye wafers and truffled pâté are gone a person might wish to wander on along the ridgetop trail toward Medra Pass (Hike 53), 2 miles distant.

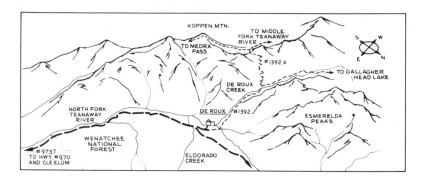

Esmerelda Peaks from Koppen Mountain

Mount Stuart from Iron Peak

NORTH FORK TEANAWAY RIVER
Unprotected area

55   IRON PEAK

Round trip to saddle 5 miles
Hiking time 4 hours
High point 6100 feet
Elevation gain 2590 feet

Hikable mid-July through
** September**
One day
USGS Mt. Stuart
Motorcycle country

If you want the Teanaway's biggest bang, viewwise, for the buck, energywise, switchback up and up a long-abandoned stock trail reopened in 1977 by the Youth Conservation Corps. The views start at the car and never quit. In early summer the same is true of the flowers.

Drive North Fork Teanaway River road (Hike 48) 9.1 miles from Stafford Creek junction, 22.6 miles from Highway 970, and park at the Iron Creek crossing, elevation 3920 feet.

The trail is all switchbacks, zigging-zagging back and forth across a rounded rib between Iron Creek on the left and Eldorado Creek on the right, usually in sound of the water but never in reach, so fill the canteens before setting out. Views begin immediately, initially only across the Teanaway valley to the gorge of De Roux Creek, soon growing to include Koppen Mountain and Esmerelda Peaks. In early summer, though, the eyes may never be raised from the ground, for in the open forest and on the open screes grows such an assortment of buckwheats and desert parsleys and orange and yellow paintbrushes as a Puget Sounder never dreamt of in his botany.

The rib fades into the hillside and the trail crosses the meadow headwaters (dry) of Eldorado Creek to a rocky saddle, 6100 feet, at 2½ miles. The trail descends from the saddle ½ mile to the Beverly–Turnpike trail, 5600 feet (Hike 51). Turn right on a boot-beaten path along the spur ridge jutting southerly from the Teanaway–Ingalls divide.

If you've never studied flowers before, start now. Little benches in the side of the ridge hold snow late and nourish an exuberance of wet-meadow plants. The serpentine barrens support the merest scattered patches of life, but these include species that grow nowhere except in serpentine soils, bringing botanists from afar to admire the rarities, some found only in this vicinity. The crazy rocks of the crest are notable for the peculiar seed pods of a very funny sort of crazyweed, as well as gorgeous cushions of violet douglasia.

As for the views, they comprehend the whole Teanaway region, Mt. Stuart the supreme lord. The bootpath ends on a broad fellfield but the next rise is a simple walk to better views of Stuart. An easy scramble over buttresses and flowers in crannied nooks leads to the summit of Iron Peak, 6510 feet.

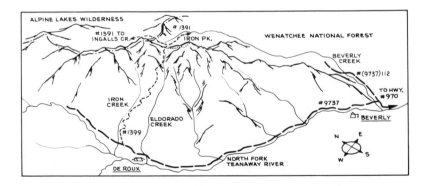

56 ESMERELDA BASIN

Round trip to Fortune Creek Pass
7 miles
Hiking time 5 hours
High point 6000 feet
Elevation gain 1750 feet
Hikable late June through
October
One day or backpack
USGS Mt. Stuart

Loop trip around Esmereldas 15
miles
Hiking time 8 hours
Elevation gain 3000 feet
Hikable July through October

Pass through a slot between craggy peaks into a peaceful basin of forests, streams, and wildflowers the more vivid for rockslide barrens. Climb to wide views at "Fortune Cookie" (Fortune Creek) Pass. Or descend through the basin from Fortune Cookie, returning from a loop trip that completely encircles Esmerelda Peaks.

Esmerelda Basin is splendid for day and weekend hikes, particularly when the Cascade Crest is misty-dripping and the sun is (maybe) brilliant here in the rainshadow. Close-to-road camps are ideal for families introducing small children to backpacking.

Drive North Fork Teanaway road (Hike 48) 10 miles from Stafford Creek junction, 23 miles from Highway 970, to the road-end at the trailhead parking lot, elevation 4243 feet.

The hike starts on a mining road built in 1910; modern-day miners do come in, but the entire basin is closed to public motor vehicles and the road now is merely a nice wide trail. Ascending within sight and sound of the creek-size river, in ¼ mile the old road passes the trail to Ingalls Lake and Longs Pass (Hikes 57 and 58). Soon the way flattens in stream-

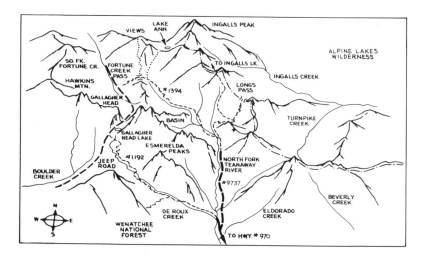

Elephant's-head (left) *and scarlet gilia* (right)

side greenery and rock gardens. Good campsites hereabouts, above and below the road; by late summer this may be the last water of the trip.

The way traverses a rocky avalanche slope, brilliant in late July with scarlet gilia and buckwheat, skirts marshy meadows covered with pink elephanthead and white bog orchid, and crosses creeks lined by violet shooting stars and blue butterwort.

At 2 miles, near fallen-down cabins of Esmerelda, the trail diverges from the old mine road and ascends to Fortune Creek Pass, 6000 feet, 3½ miles. For bigger views climb the righthand (north) skyline to a 6500-foot hilltop. Or, drop back down from the pass ¼ mile to the last creek and ascend it to a hidden basin and a pass overlooking Lake Ann, a delightful tarn (Hike 52).

Fortune Creek Pass via the loop: At 1½ miles short of the road-end, park where the sideroad drops left to what used to be De Roux Forest Camp, elevation 3750 feet. In the camp find the De Roux Creek trail (Hike 54) and follow it over the river and up a spectacular gorge; in 1 mile, just beyond a crossing of the creek, keep right at the junction with trail No. 1394A. The way passes lewisia rockeries and levels out in a meadow basin with delightful camps. Switchbacks climb to the broad, green vale between crags of Esmerelda Peaks and Hawkins Mountain. There, at 5600 feet, *bad news:* The Forest Service has left open to jeep jockeys the old mining track that comes up Boulder Creek and goes down Fortune Creek. In a few yards, 4 miles from the road, emerge in emerald lawns around pretty little Gallagher Head Lake—and see wheel tracks trenching marshy meadows. Follow the road down from the lake 1 mile, at about 5050 feet spot the path taking off uphill right, and switchback 1 mile to Fortune Creek Pass. On the survey day in late July more than 150 species of flowers were in bloom on the loop.

57 INGALLS LAKE

Round trip to Ingalls Lake 9 miles
Hiking time 8 hours
High point 6500 feet
Elevation gain 2600 feet in, 600
feet out

Hikable mid-July through
mid-October
One day or backpack
USGS Mt. Stuart

A rock-basin lake at the foot of rugged Ingalls Peak, at the top of waterfalls plunging to Ingalls Creek, and directly across the valley from the massive south wall of 9415-foot Mt. Stuart, the highest peak between

Ingalls Lake and Mount Stuart

Glacier Peak and Rainier. The blend of blue lake, snowfields, ice-polished slabs of brown rock, lush green meadows, a glory of flowers, and groves of whitebark pine, larch, and subalpine fir is magical.

Drive to the end of the North Fork Teanaway road, elevation 4243 feet, and hike to Esmerelda Basin (Hike 56). At ¼ mile turn right on the trail signed for Longs Pass and Ingalls Lake. Carry a loaded canteen; the climb can be hot and often is waterless.

The path ascends steadily in fields of grass and blossoms, patches of small trees. Nearby ridges are a startling blend of gray and brown and rusty-red rocks. South beyond Esmerelda Peaks appear Mt. Adams, the Goat Rocks, and Mt. Rainier. At 5600 feet is a junction; the right fork climbs a scant ½ mile to 6250-foot Longs Pass (Hike 58). Go left, swinging around the mountainside into a small valley, winding through buttresses and flowers, joining an older and steeper trail. Just below the pass is a small, green bench with snowmelt (and camps) in early summer. The final stretch switchbacks to Ingalls Pass, 6500 feet, 3 miles, and a grand view of Mt. Stuart. The way to here is mostly free of snow in late June, while slopes to the north are still white. The ridge can be scrambled in either direction for higher views.

Contour left on slopes above Headlight Creek Basin, a parkland with cold streams and delightful camps. The way enters a lovely little hanging basin, crosses its creek, descends a bit, then climbs a low ridge of polished brown buttresses—and at last, below is the lake. The way down to the 6463-foot shore is short and easy, but getting around the west (lefthand) side to the outlet requires a ticklish scramble up and down slabs and huge boulders. Don't try the righthand side—it's strictly a rock-climbing route.

From the outlet one can explore to Stuart Pass (Hike 43).

Camping is very limited here and firewood nonexistent: anyhow, the lake basin is extremely overused and should be considered a "day use zone." Camp either in Headlight Creek Basin or below the lake in meadowy headwaters of Ingalls Creek.

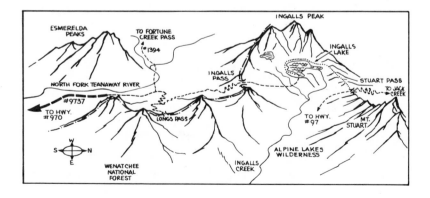

Mount Stuart from Longs Pass

NORTH FORK TEANAWAY RIVER
Unprotected area

LONGS PASS

Round trip 5 miles
Hiking time 3 hours
High point 6300 feet
Elevation gain 2100 feet

Hikable July through October
One day
USGS Mt. Stuart

Longs Pass is the best seat in the house, front row center, for the big show of 9415-foot Mt. Stuart, without a rival between Rainier and Glacier. Day hikes are the general choice, spending an awed lunchtime gazing across the gulf of Ingalls Creek to the granite cleavers and walls, searching with binoculars for goats and climbers. In idiot times of the not-too-distant past, as soon as machines were built that could do it, prospectors gouged a cat track to the pass, largely obliterating the old trail. However, a new route has been neatly switchbacked and the hike is the most popular in the area.

Drive to the end of North Fork Teanaway River road, elevation 4243 feet, and set out on Esmerelda Basin trail No. 1394 (Hike 56). In ¼ mile turn off right on Ingalls Lake–Longs Pass trail No. 1390.

The sparse forest permits views north into Esmerelda Basin and west to Esmerelda Peaks. Trees pretty well give up the struggle to live in the serpentine soils, deficient as they are in certain essential minerals and vitamins, and only plants that can adapt to a poor diet and little water spatter the naked earth with dusty greenery and brilliant blossoms. During the steady, steep ascent the views change abruptly at each switchback as boots and eyes are pointed north to barren red-rock basins, then south to the rugged lichen-dark cliffs.

At 2 miles, 5600 feet, the trail splits. Lake Ingalls trail (Hike 57) goes left; go right on trail No. 1229, switchbacking onward and upward over talus, briefly joining the old bulldozer track and, when it heads straight up the slope, resuming a civilized zigzag. At 2½ miles the way crosses a bench with several nice campsites (no water after the snowmelt dries) and quickly attains Longs Pass, 6300 feet.

Climbers commonly camp here to make the ascent of the "dog route" up Stuart, usually in late spring when snow is abundant for cooking into water on stoves. They then descend to Ingalls Creek on remains of an ancient trail or simply plunge down the snow, over talus and through forest. Or they may camp at Ingalls Creek, 4800 feet.

Hikers rarely have any good reason to do that and, if they wish more exercise, scramble the ridge crest north a ways or, in cases of terminal eagerness and a degree of mountaineering skill, traverse the 6878-foot peak and drop to Ingalls Pass (a loop!). Those of milder disposition may follow the bulldozer track south along the ridge 1000 feet and drop to a secluded basin, pleasant camping while the snowmelt lasts.

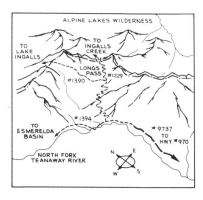

Columbine

Mount Rainier from Elbow Peak

MIDDLE FORK TEANAWAY RIVER
Unprotected area

59 YELLOW HILL– ELBOW PEAK

Round trip to Elbow Peak 10 miles
Hiking time 5 hours
High point 5673 feet
Elevation gain 2800 feet in, 300 feet out

Hikable mid-June through October
One day
USGS Mt. Stuart and Kachess Lake
Motorcycle country

Even by Teanaway standards the views are outstanding from the sky-open ridge between Yellow Hill and Elbow Peak, the panorama of the Alpine Lakes Wilderness stretching from Mt. Stuart east of the Cascade Crest to Overcoat Peak west of it. The toil up the steep, dry trail is forgotten on the summit, though perhaps not the snarl and whine of the motorcycles ridden here by those who love to feel the wind blow in one ear and out the other.

Drive the Teanaway River road (Hike 48) 7.6 miles from Highway 970 and go left on Middle Fork road No. 113. In .7 mile the road forks; stay right. In 2.6 miles pavement ends. At 4.6 miles pass the Middle Fork trail and in another .3 mile turn right on a very rough road to Yellow Hill trail. The hiking mileages here are from road No. 113, elevation 3200 feet.

Wheels with various combinations of wheels, tires, and drive trains go one distance or another, but at 1 mile the trail suddenly appears, heading steeply up the ridge crest while the road makes a switchback, the two rejoining briefly and splitting, the trail to make another lightning ascent while the road switchbacks. At 1½ miles they rejoin again, crest a ridge overlooking the Middle Fork Teanaway valley, and here the road finally gives it up, at 4400 feet.

The trail, now molested only by two-wheelers, heads out along the ridge through open pine forest, traversing the west side of Yellow Hill, at 2 miles suddenly veering upward in great contour-leaping strides. While pausing to gasp and shift gears, enjoy the view south over the Middle Fork and West Fork valleys to the main Teanaway River and on out to the Yakima River.

At 3 miles Mt. Rainier comes in view, so enormous it seems very near. In ¼ mile more the trail abruptly levels out to contour around Yellow Hill just below the summit, 5500 feet. The way swings to the north slope of the hill, views excellent of Elbow Peak and Jolly Mountain dead ahead and Stuart to the northeast, drops 300 feet to a saddle, and resumes climbing along a thin ridge.

In the final ½ mile the path nearly disappears in the rocks, which include striking veins of calcite crystals, before the last push up to the grassy summit of Elbow Peak, 5 miles, 5673 feet.

It's far enough for the day. However, the imaginative will note with interest that the trail continues along the ridge 3½ miles to Jolly Mountain (Hike 65), connecting to trails from Salmon la Sac.

Middle Fork Teanaway road   Old:
                                    New: 113

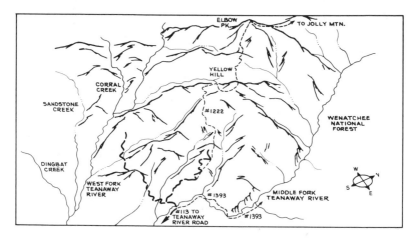

60   KACHESS RIDGE

One-way trip 14¾ miles
Hiking time 8 hours
High point 5854 feet
Elevation gain 2600 feet

Hikable July through
   mid-October
One day or backpack
USGS Kachess Lake
Motorcycle country

An island of wildland isolated by reservoirs west and east, logging roads north, and freeway south is a proper candidate for a wilderness designation all its own, the ridge climaxed by cliffs and flowers of Thorp Mountain, the views the same (if one can mentally erase reservoirs, clearcuts, and powerlines) as explorers saw a century ago—Rainier, Stuart, Daniels, and the jagged array of Dutch Miller peaks. It's a one-way trip, requiring the arrangement of transportation at each end. Logic dictates starting at the high end rather than the low, and so the route is here described.

To leave a car at the lower trailhead, drive Interstate 90 east 16.8 miles from Snoqualmie Pass, go off on Lake Easton State Park Exit 70, cross to the north side of the freeway, and turn left on Sparks road, following "Lake Kachess Dam" signs. In .5 mile take a right on road No. 4818 and in .4 mile another right on the powerline road. At the first junction keep left to reach the trailhead in 1 mile, elevation 2350 feet.

To begin the trip, drive Interstate 90 to Salmon la Sac–Roslyn Exit 80 and proceed through Roslyn and Ronald and along Lake Cle Elum. At 15 miles from Roslyn, a mile short of Salmon la Sac Campground, turn left on Cooper Lake road No. 46, cross the Cle Elum River, and drive 4.7 miles to Cooper Lake junction. Keep straight ahead on road No. 4600 to Cooper Pass, about 9 miles, and turn left on road No. (4600)125, climbing steeply 2 more miles to trail No. 1315, elevation 3700 feet.

The trail works its way up through a clearcut then enters forest, switchbacking up and over a wooded 4826-foot knoll on No Name Ridge,

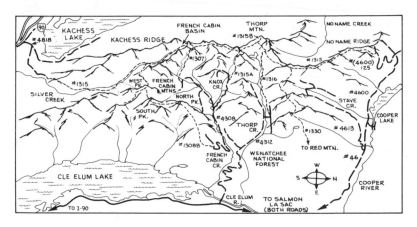

Kachess Ridge

and with few views follows the ridge's ups and downs. At 4 miles cross a 5487-foot hump and pass a junction with Red Mountain trail No. 1330. The way traverses steep slopes on the east side of Thorp Mountain, at 4½ miles passing Thorp Creek trail No. 1316 and at 4¾ miles reaching Thorp Mountain trail No. 1315B. The short sidetrip is mandatory to flowers and views atop Thorp Mountain, 5854 feet (Hike 61).

The ridge trail continues along a narrow crest, climbs steeply, at 5¼ miles passes Knox Creek trail No. 1315A, goes upsy-downsy by French Cabin Creek trail No. 1307 at 7¼ miles, traverses to a saddle between Kachess Ridge and the west peak of French Cabin Mountain, and enters headwaters of Silver Creek. At 9 miles is trail No. 1308B, near possible camps. The path continues down, at 14¾ miles coming to the south trailhead.

Cooper Lake road	Old:	228	Old:	2105	2218
	New:	46	New:	4818	4600(125)
Cooper Pass road	Old:	229			
	New:	4600			

61 THORP MOUNTAIN

Round trip 9 miles
Hiking time 7½ hours
High point 5850 feet
Elevation gain 2750 feet in, 600
feet out

Hikable late July through
mid-October
One day
USGS Kachess Lake
Motorcycle country

Magnificent trail country of forest ridges and green meadows climaxing at Thorp Mountain Lookout. Views—Rainier, Stuart, Daniel, and the Dutch Miller Gap peaks. Other views, less esthetic—Kachess Lake (reservoir), powerlines, logging roads (which have shrunk the wildland and brought the ridge in easy reach of a day hike).

The Kachess Ridge trail extends 14¾ miles from road No. 4818 near Easton to near Cooper Pass (Hike 60). The shortest route to Thorp Mountain is Knox Creek trail No. 1315A, starting at 4000 feet and meeting the

Thorp Mountain Lookout

Kachess Ridge trail in 1½ miles: the total distance to the lookout is 2½ miles, gaining 1800 feet. The way is fairly straightforward, climbing almost entirely in meadows of blueberries and flowers. Described here is the French Cabin Creek trail, longer and with more ups and downs but giving views of the French Cabin Mountains, a panorama of the Knox Creek trail country, and eventually winding up in the same place.

Drive the Salmon la Sac road 12 miles from the City Hall, First and Dakota, in Roslyn. Just past the end of Cle Elum Lake (reservoir) turn left on French Cabin Creek road No. 4308 and drive 7 miles to the trailhead. On the way pass Knox Creek road No. 4312 at 5 miles (Knox Creek trail starts 2 miles up this road) and at an unmarked junction at 6 miles keep to the right side of the stream. The actual trailhead is up a short, rough spur; it may be best to park on the road, elevation 3700 feet.

French Cabin Creek trail No. 1305 starts in a clearcut and continues in an old burn. At spots very steep, at 1 mile it reaches a campsite with a good spring, ascends more clearcuts and skirts a road, and at 1½ miles joins the Kachess Ridge trail (6½ miles from road No. 4818 near Easton). The ridge trail now grows extremely steep as it ascends a 5700-foot hump at 2 miles. The south side of this high point has great views back over the French Cabin peaks, Kachess Lake, and Rainier. At the start of the descent of the north side is a view down on Knox Creek trail.

From the high point the trail drops steeply 400 feet, contours a peak, passes Knox Creek trail at 3¾ miles, climbs, drops 200 feet, climbs another high point, and comes out atop a ridge bump 500 feet directly above Thorp Lake. At 4¼ miles is a junction with the Thorp Mountain trail, which switchbacks 400 feet to the lookout at 4½ miles.

The ridge trail proceeds 6½ more miles to road No. (4600)125 near Cooper Pass.

French Cabin Creek road	Old:	2211	Old:	2105
	New:	4308	New:	4818
Knox Creek road	Old:	2211B		
	New:	4312		

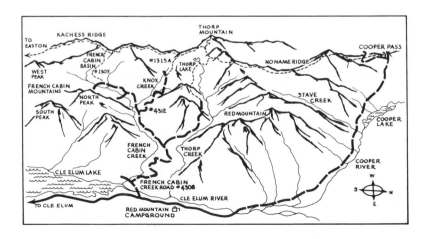

62   SPECTACLE LAKE

Round trip 18½ miles
Allow 2 days
High point 4350 feet
Elevation gain 1550 feet

Hikable August through
September
USGS Snoqualmie Pass and
Kachess Lake

Only a scattering of miniature glaciers remains of the huge frozen streams that gouged out the Alpine Lakes region of the Cascades. However, the handiwork of ancient ice lies everywhere and is beautifully exhibited by this delightful lake in a basin of glacier-polished rock.

Drive Interstate 90 to Salmon la Sac–Roslyn Exit 80 and proceed through Roslyn and Ronald and along Cle Elum Lake. At 15 miles from Roslyn, a mile short of Salmon la Sac Campground, turn left on Cooper River road No. 46, cross the Cle Elum River, and drive 4.7 miles to Cooper Lake junction. Turn right on Cooper Lake road No. 4616 past the recreation area and turn left on road No. (4616)113 a final 1 mile to the trailhead, elevation 2800 feet.

Cooper River trail No. 1323 joins the lakeshore path starting at the campground and follows the Cooper River, rippling beautifully through virgin forest, 5½ miles to Pete Lake, 2980 feet, and much-used and often-crowded campsites. Unravel a confusion of paths at the shelter cabin and find the main trail, which climbs slightly over a rocky rib and drops to a double crossing of two swift creeks at about 7 miles. Both must be crossed. Footlogs may be available; if not, boulder hopping can be difficult in the high water of early summer. When water is impossibly high, follow Lemah Meadow trail No. 1323B some ¾ mile to the Pacific Crest Trail, which crosses the creeks on bridges; the detour adds 1 mile each way.

Shortly beyond the two creeks, join the Pacific Crest Trail and switchback up toward Chikamin Ridge, mostly in forest, views scarce. At 8¾

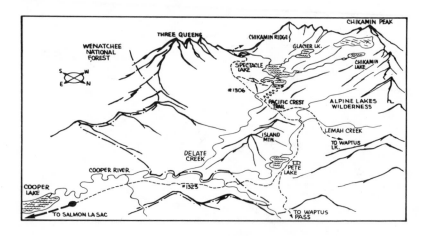

Spectacle Lake and Chikamin Ridge

miles the Crest Trail proceeds onward toward Spectacle Point and Park
Lakes and the first of two Spectacle Lake trails branches right.

This first path, called the Staircase because it climbs straight up with
trees and roots for footholds, is strenuous but only ½ mile long and com-
pensates by passing a lovely waterfall spilling from the lake, 4350 feet.
For the best camps (carry a stove—no fires allowed) cross the outlet just
above the falls and walk the south shore. The lake is like an octopus with
a half-dozen arms, which makes the shoreline difficult to traverse but
provides many glorious camps. To the south rises Three Queens, about
6800 feet. To the northwest is Chikamin Peak and to the north the spectacular spires of 7512-foot Lemah Mountain.

Simply poking about on slabs and buttresses of the lakeshore, admiring polishings and groovings done by the ice and picturesque groupings
of trees, can fill out a leisurely visit. But one really ought not miss the
smashing views from Spectacle Point. Thread through the confusing
maze of upsy-downsy paths south, eventually ending up on the sidetrail
that ½ mile from the lake outlet hits the Pacific Crest Trail at ¾ mile
from The Staircase start. This second access to the lake adds 1¼ miles to
the approach and a good bit of extra elevation is gained and lost, but the
walking is easier. Climb 2 miles to the high-in-the-sky viewpoint, 5475
feet. If ambition continues, proceed on to the next pass (Hike 82).

| Cooper River road | Old: | 229 | Cooper Lake road | Old: | 235 |
| | New: | 46 | | New: | 4616 |

63 TIRED CREEK– POLALLIE RIDGE

Round trip to ridge top 11 miles
Hiking time 7 hours
High point 5360 feet
Elevation gain 2600 feet

Hikable late June through
  October
One day
USGS Lake Kachess

Splendid views are to be had from this high ridge, and though the trail is dry (look to your canteens, troopers) the mouth will water when the eyes drink in Cooper Lake, Dutch Miller Gap's bold rock peaks, and ice-creamy Mt. Hinman and Mt. Daniel, the latter famed as the highest peak in King County.

Drive to the Cooper River trailhead, elevation 2800 feet (Hike 62).

Follow Pete Lake trail No. 1323 along the Cooper River 1 flat mile and turn right and up on Tired Creek trail No. 1317. In a long ¼ mile cross an abandoned logging road and be guided by signs on a bulldozed fire trail climbing steeply around a clearcut and at the top joining the old trail, a rough but adequate path ascending steadily with many switchbacks. Views begin at the road and get better as elevation is gained. At about 1¾ miles two switchbacks on the edge of a ridge offer a look west to Pete Lake. At 2 miles forest yields to meadowlands as the trail traverses under the ridge and aims for a wooded pass at the head of Tired Creek.

The best views are from the top of this ridge, a logical turnaround for day hikers and an absolutely mandatory sidetrip for those continuing on. Leave the trail at any convenient spot, scramble to the crest, and walk to the highest point, 5360 feet, a great place to soak up scenery and spend the day watching shadows move along distant mountains.

Many goodies remain in store for hikers choosing to continue. Descend from the view crest to regain the trail and contour to the wooded pass, 5280 feet, 3 miles from the abandoned logging road, and a bit beyond to a junction. The left fork drops 2 miles to Waptus Pass; for a 15-mile loop

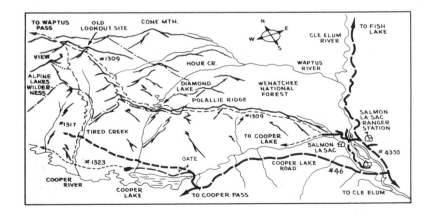

Pete Lake, Chikamin Peak (left), *Lemah Mountain* (right), *from Polallie Ridge*

trip, return to the car via this pass and Pete Lake (Hike 62).

The right fork climbs a scant ¼ mile to the site of the old Polallie Ridge lookout, 5482 feet. Amid fragrant meadows settle down to swig the jug of raspberry punch and eat a Cadbury with cashews while gazing all around to magnificent mountains and deep, green valleys.

For a different loop, continue on Pollalie Ridge trail 5½ miles downhill, then the Cooper River trail 3½ miles upstream (Hikes 69 and 66), returning to the campground at Cooper Lake and thence to your car for a total loop of 16 miles.

64 MINERAL CREEK PARK

**Round trip from Cooper Pass
   road 10 miles
Hiking time 8 hours
High point 4700 feet
Elevation gain 2300 feet
Hikable July through October
One day or backpack**

**USGS Snoqualmie Pass and
   Kachess Lake**

**Round trip from Kachess Lake
   Campground 20 miles
Allow 2 days
Elevation gain 3300 feet**

Heather and huckleberry meadows surrounding alpine lakes, mountains to climb, and views. The trail is tough and not many fish are in the lakes, so the area currently offers more solitude than nearby Spectacle and Rachel Lakes.

Once upon a time—until 1968, in fact—the trip began with a lovely walk along Kachess Lake. Now, in the name of progress, a logging road has intersected the route right in the middle, cutting the hike in half. Since the challenge and satisfaction of traveling the entire distance in unmarred wilderness have been lost, the most practical plan probably is to use the new road as an approach to the upper half and maybe some other day walk the lower half.

To reach the halfway point, drive to Cooper Lake (Hike 62) and keep left on road No. 4600, climbing over Cooper Pass and dropping into the Kachess valley. At about 11 miles from the Cle Elum River road find the trailhead, elevation 2400 feet, amid a confusion of Burlington-Northern clearcut. (The Forest Service plans to place markers to guide hikers.)

Just in case there are die-hard hikers willing to ignore the new road to recapture a semblance of the old wilderness experience, the trip from Kachess Lake will be described here.

Drive Interstate 90 east from Snoqualmie Pass 12½ miles, take

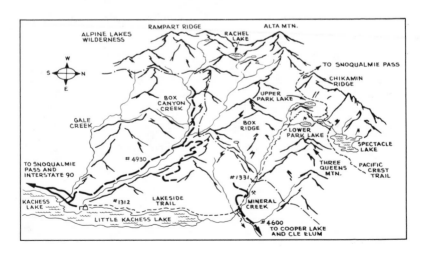

Upper Park Lake

Kachess Lake Exit 62, and follow signs 5 miles to Kachess Lake Campground. Inside the campground proceed .7 mile to the northernmost (uplake) section and follow signs to the trailhead, elevation 2254 feet.

Little Kachess trail No. 1312 follows the lake more than 3 miles to its head, never over 200–400 feet above the water, but seldom level and with so many ups and downs that about 1000 feet of elevation are gained and lost. At the end of the lake the footpath merges into a mining road built in the days of the Model T and now abandoned. At about 4½ miles the route turns up Mineral Creek trail No. 1331, climbing steeply; here is the junction with the logging road, the beginning of the short version of the trip.

The mining road continues 1¼ miles to an end at a group of dilapidated buildings; until the Alpine Lakes Wilderness boundary is crossed, expect complications from Burlington-Northern. From here on the tread mainly just grew, going up and down and around, never flat, often very steep. Most of the way is brushed out—thankfully so, for much of the route is on slopes of slick alder and vine maple. Beyond the mine buildings ¼ mile the trail crosses Mineral Creek and at about 3¾ miles from the Cooper Pass logging road crosses the outlet stream from lower Park Lake. At about 5 miles the path reaches upper Park Lake, 4700 feet, and the edge of meadow country. Excellent camps here (no wood fires permitted); more are ½ mile to the west up a small stream.

Actually, the lakes are nice but not exceptional, not for *this* area. For the truly memorable trip continue ¼ mile up to intersect the Pacific Crest Trail at 4970 feet. Climb left to a pass or right to Spectacle Point for great views (Hike 82). Roam hillocks and vales of the headwater basin on way trails and maybe find the goat path over Box Ridge to Lila Lakes.

65 JOLLY MOUNTAIN

Round trip from Salmon la Sac 12 miles
Hiking time 7–8 hours
High point 6443 feet
Elevation gain 4043 feet

Hikable July through September
One day
USGS Kachess Lake

An eastern outpost of the Alpine Lakes Cascades with 360-degree views east to Mt. Stuart and the freeway leading into Ellensburg, north to Mt. Daniel, west to Pete Lake and the Dutch Miller Gap peaks, south to Mt. Rainier, and directly down to Cle Elum Lake.

Drive Interstate 90 to Salmon la Sac–Roslyn Exit 80 and proceed through Roslyn and Ronald, beside Cle Elum Lake, and at 16 miles from Roslyn reach the community of Salmon la Sac. Shortly before an historic old log building turn right on a road to the trailhead parking area by the Forest Service horse barn, elevation 2400 feet.

Go to the left side of the barn and find the trailhead at the edge of the public corral. In ¼ mile briefly touch a service road and then return to trail, which climbs steeply with many switchbacks to a difficult crossing (easier by late July) of Salmon la Sac Creek. This is the only certain water on the entire route. At 3½ miles is a junction with the Paris Creek trail; keep right. The way ascends the valley a bit farther and then starts a series of switchbacks up the hillside. At 4½ miles is a junction with the

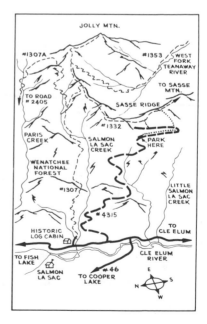

Yellow bell

Mount Stuart from Jolly Mountain

Sasse Mountain sheep driveway (to use this as an alternate approach, see below). Keep left ¼ mile to a junction with the unmarked Jolly Creek trail. Go right, climbing steeply amid growing views for the final 1¼ miles to the 6443-foot summit, site of a fire lookout removed in 1968.

A jolly place to sop up panoramas. Carry a state road map to identify landmarks far out in Eastern Washington and a Forest Service map to name the innumerable peaks.

Though there may be snowfields to traverse then and the creek is difficult to cross, a magnificent time for the trip is June, when the way lies through fields of glacier lilies, spreading phlox, and lanceleaf spring beauty. Unfortunately, a band of sheep occasionally summers in the area and some of the meadows may be close-cropped.

An alternate approach saves about 1500 feet of climbing—at the cost of ½ mile or more of off-trail travel. Just .6 mile south of Salmon la Sac find Little Salmon la Sac road No. 4315 (closed in some seasons) and drive 4½ miles to an elevation of about 4500 feet. Park on a turnout near the road-end. It is best to walk the road near its end and then climb straight up the hill to intersect the Sasse Mountain sheep driveway on the crest of Sasse Ridge. The forested slopes are steep but mostly brushfree. Be sure to mark the spot where the ridge is reached in order to retrace steps on the return. Follow the sheep trail north a little over a mile to the junction with the Salmon la Sac trail and proceed to the top of Jolly Mountain.

If transportation can be arranged, a good loop trip can be made by going up the Little Salmon la Sac road and down the Jolly Mountain trail.

Little Salmon la Sac road   Old: 2216
                              New: 4315

Cooper Lake

CLE ELUM RIVER
Unprotected area

 # COOPER RIVER

One-way trip to Cooper Lake 4 miles
Hiking time 2 hours
High point 2800 feet
Elevation gain 400 feet

Hikable June through October
One day or backpack
USGS Lake Kachess

Solitude and untrammeled, untrampled wilderness—this is not the hike for that. The forest path along rocky banks of the swift-flowing

Cooper River is thronged with enthusiastic Scouts, families, large groups of friends, twosomes, and singles enjoying sauntering walks or picnics, watching the birds, watching the water, studying flowers and trees, and generally having a good time. Part of the fun of this trip is seeing how much fun people have on a trail. Wear a happy face and make friends.

Drive to Salmon la Sac (Hike 65) and cross the Cle Elum River bridge. Just beyond, at the campground entrance and to the west of the Waptus River trail (Hike 67), find Cooper River trail No. 1311, elevation 2400 feet. (Logging may move the trailhead ¼ mile up the Cooper River, in which event the road to the trail will be well-signed.)

The trail skirts Salmon la Sac Campground, passes private cabins, and in ¼ mile reaches Cooper River and turns upstream. Viewpoints of the river beckon. Green pools invite. At ½ mile, 2480 feet, Polallie Ridge trail No. 1309 (Hikes 63 and 69) branches right; it, too, may be disrupted by logging to come.

In the next mile the path gains 300 feet, then remains nearly level to the lake, weaving through trees. At 2½ miles the way diverges from the river to cross a small creek from Polallie Ridge and returns to the river. From the far side come occasional sounds of vehicles on the Cooper River road. At 4 miles the trail crosses road No. 4616 and drops into Owhi Campground on the shores of Cooper Lake, 2788 feet, a good turnaround for day hikers; whether a backpacker would care to bed down here among the car campers is questionable.

A common way to exploit the trail as a one-way trip is for part of a family or group to drive to the lake for a picnic, the rest to walk there. All or some of this group (or any other) may be pleased to take the 3-mile around-the-lake trail, with a degree of solitude and nice views over the water to forested ridges.

Cooper River road   Old: 235
                    New: 4616

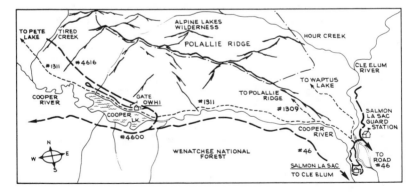

67 WAPTUS RIVER

**Round trip to Waptus Lake 18
  miles
Allow 2 days
High point 2963 feet
Elevation gain about 1000 feet,
  including ups and downs**

**Hikable July through October
USGS Kachess Lake and Mt.
  Daniel**

The largest lake in the Alpine Lakes region, about 2 miles long and ⅜ mile wide, lying in a glacier-carved valley and reflecting the spectacular spire of 7197-foot Bears Breast Mountain and snowfields on Summit Chief Mountain. The approach is entirely through forest, mainly young trees growing up after some long-forgotten fire. The lake is great, but only the beginning of good things all the way to the valley head at Dutch Miller Gap on the Cascade Crest.

Drive to Salmon la Sac (Hike 65) and cross the Cle Elum River bridge. Just beyond, at the edge of the campground, find the head of Waptus River trail No. 1310, elevation 2400 feet.

The route starts on a private road past a group of summer homes, then begins a gradual ascent, first on remnants of a road used years ago for selective logging, soon becoming genuine trail. At 2 miles, 3000 feet, top the low divide and drop to the Waptus valley floor at the easy ford of Hour Creek, about 3 miles. The camp here is rather horsey; hikers will be happier in any of the numerous small riverside sites up the valley.

The trail now climbs 300 feet, again drops a little, and at about 4 miles touches the bank of the Waptus River. Views here of 5295-foot Cone Mountain rising above the route ahead. The way henceforth remains close to the river, whose clear waters sometimes dance over boulders, other times flow so quietly and smoothly they seem not to move at all.

At about 6 miles the trail rounds the base of Cone Mountain, opening views toward the head of the valley, and at 8½ miles reaches a junction. The left fork leads along the west shore of Waptus Lake and climbs Polallie Ridge (Hike 69) to Waptus Pass and Pete Lake (Hike 62).

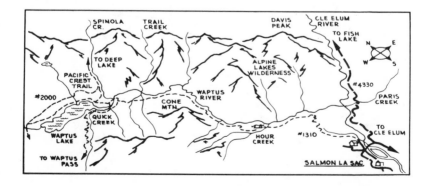

Summit Chief Mountain (left), *Bears Breast Mountain* (right), *from Waptus Lake*

The Waptus trail goes right, turning downvalley ¼ mile to a steel-and-wood bridge over the river, then heading upvalley again to cross Spinola Creek and join Spinola Creek trail No. 1310A coming from Deep Lake (Hike 75). At 9 miles the path arrives at Waptus Lake, 2963 feet, and a wonderful campsite with the best views of mountains reflected in water. However, this is also the most crowded camp; for other lakeside sites follow the trail 1½ miles along the shore.

The trail continues up the Waptus valley, ascending moderately for 3½ miles; along the way, at Spade Creek, it joins the Pacific Crest Trail and the two proceed as one to the Upper Waptus River bridge. Here the gentle climbing ends. As the Crest Trail goes off left to switchback up Escondido Ridge, Dutch Miller Gap trail No. 1362 goes right, switchbacking 1400 feet in 2½ miles to Lake Ivanhoe at 4652 feet, 15 miles from the road. At 16 miles the trail reaches the 5000-foot summit of Dutch Miller Gap (Hike 96).

68 SPADE LAKE

Round trip from the road 28 miles
Allow 3 days
High point 5400 feet
Elevation gain 3400 feet
Hikable mid-July through
   September
USGS Mt. Daniel

Round trip from Waptus Lake 8
   miles
Hiking time 6 hours
Elevation gain 2400 feet

A high and very beautiful alpine lake under the tall southern buttresses of Mt. Daniel. The deep blue waters, generally frozen until the middle of July, are surrounded by bare, rounded rock with striations that tell the story of the glacier that carved this cirque from the side of Mt. Daniel not so many thousand years ago.

The Spade Lake trail, originally a sheep driveway, is extremely steep and badly eroded and lies on a south-facing slope, which though largely shaded can be hot and dry; on sunny days set out from Waptus Lake no later than 7 a.m. The approximately 4-mile route takes from 3 to 5 hours up and 2 to 3 hours down—and to get to the beginning one must first hike 10 miles up the Waptus River.

Drive to Salmon la Sac and hike to Waptus Lake (Hike 67). Follow the trail around the north shore a short mile and at 10 miles from the road find Spade Lake trail No. 1337, elevation 3000 feet.

The trail is rough and steep as it climbs rapidly, crossing the Pacific Crest Trail, and becomes rougher and steeper as it shoots straight up the hillside, gaining 1200 feet in about 1½ miles to 4200 feet. The climb then

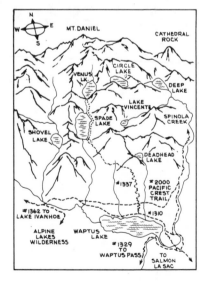

White heather

Glacier-polished rock at the outlet of Spade Lake

eases, alternating between steep climbing, maddening short descents, and an occasional brief contour. The path remains difficult but the views improve, including an aerial perspective down on Waptus Lake. The first reliable water is at 2½ miles, 5200 feet. At 3 miles, 5400 feet, is a dramatic view of the summit spire of Bears Breast rising above great, smooth cliffs, and of glaciers on 7300-foot Summit Chief. The Dutch Miller Gap trail can be seen switchbacking up the opposite hillside. About now one can loop ahead to glacier-polished rock at the outlet of Spade Lake and to the southern cliffs of Mt. Hinman, with a small piece of glacier showing. A last rugged mile of many little ups and downs leads to the lake at 5210 feet.

Campsites are located near the outlet, on a peninsula halfway around the south shore, and in heather meadows above the lake. The meadows are ribbed by outcrops of polished rock, making travel slow. Don't camp on the heather—once broken down it takes years to regrow.

A worthwhile sidetrip is Venus Lake, 5672 feet. Follow a fishermen's path ¾ mile along the east side of Spade Lake and climb the rocks just to the right of the waterfall another ¾ mile. Except for the narrow outlet (room for several campers) Venus Lake is surrounded by tall, naked cliffs.

69   WAPTUS PASS LOOP

Basic loop 21 miles
Allow 2–4 days
High point 5547 feet
Elevation gain 3147 feet

Hikable mid-July through
    mid-September
USGS Kachess Lake

Here's a loop to pump up a connoisseur of looping. Link the Waptus River trail to the Cooper River trail via the green meadows of Waptus Pass and the wide-view heights of Polallie Ridge. Add a couple of extra days to extend the loop to one or more subalpine lakes and another high vista from a rib of Summit Chief Mountain.

Drive to Salmon la Sac (Hike 65) and cross the Cle Elum River bridge. Just beyond, at the campground edge, find Waptus River trail No. 1310 (Hike 67), elevation 2400 feet. (Logging may require relocation of this trailhead and that for Pollalie Ridge, in which case signs will point the new ways.)

Hike along the Waptus River, passing excellent camps at 3 and 6½ miles, to where the horse and foot trails to 2963-foot Waptus Lake diverge at 8¼ miles. Good camps lie ¾ mile along both trails. Those on the footpath have splendid views of Bears Breast and Summit Chief Mountains and Dutch Miller Gap but usually are very busy. Those on the horse-ford path are more secluded but less scenic and somewhat horsey.

The loop route follows the horse trail ½ mile to a split where the beasts turn right to ford the river; go left ¼ mile to another fork. The right fork leads ¼ mile to lakeshore camps; go left and steeply ascend the forested gorge of Quick Creek. At 2 miles from the lake the angle eases and at 3 miles are marshy meadows of Waptus Pass, 4320 feet. Here is a trail junction, the right to Escondido Lake and the Waptus Burn trail and the left, the loop route, to Polallie Ridge. The pass has two nice camps, one just before the junction and one just beyond.

The Polallie Ridge trail, boggy in spots and with some windfall, ascends the crest, in woods and opens, 1½ miles to Tired Creek trail (Hike 63) from the Cooper River, and ¼ mile more to the site of Polallie Ridge

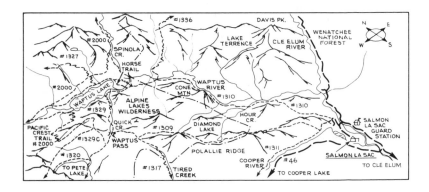

164

Cathedral Rock and Mount Daniel from Polallie Ridge

Lookout, 5482 feet. This is the climax vista of the loop, so get out the squirrel food and banana chips and count the major summits: Cathedral Rock, Daniel, Hinman, Bears Breast, Summit Chief, Overcoat, Chimney Rock, Lemah, Chikamin, Three Queens, and, of course, Rainier.

Beyond the lookout site ½ mile the trail passes the highest, but forested, point of the ridge, 5547 feet, and shortly splits. The left fork is the official line of descent, the right a bootpath that remains on the crest another ¼ mile to milk the last panoramas and plunge to the main trail, which drops to a marshy bench on the east slope of the ridge, reclimbs the crest, and repeats the procedure. The third descent reaches Diamond Lake, 5060 feet, 4½ miles from Waptus Pass, and several small camps.

The way climbs over one final rib and begins the long run down the lowering crest of Polallie Ridge to the foot, where Cooper River trail (Hike 66), leads ½ mile back to Salmon la Sac.

Variations on the basic loop: From Waptus Lake hike the Pacific Crest Trail 6½ miles to a 5700-foot shoulder of Summit Chief, then Waptus Burn trail No. 1329C for 2½ miles to Waptus Pass. Or, stay on the Crest Trail a mile beyond this junction, take the bootpath down to Escondido Lake, follow the rather marshy trail to the Pete Lake trail, and return to the basic loop at Waptus Pass. Or if too dizzy to stop looping, let your imagination run wild all the way to Pete Lake and wherever.

70 DAVIS PEAK

Round trip 11 miles
Hiking time 8 hours
High point 6426 feet
Elevation gain 3900 feet

Hikable (in part) May through
October
One day
USGS Kachess Lake

A long, hot, dry hike in open forest, repaid by views of the Snoqualmie peaks, Mt. Daniel, and forests of the Waptus valley from a lookout peak overlooking the Salmon la Sac region. The eastern slopes of the Cascades often have sunshine while the westside peaks are lost in clouds, so start in early morning.

Drive to Salmon la Sac (Hike 65) and about 2 miles more. Cross Paris Creek bridge, go 500 feet, turn left and down past private residences. Beyond the last cabin avoid the obvious road which curves to the right and down the hill. Instead, at the center of the curve turn left over the bank to another roadway (marked by a small sign "Bridge Trail") which leads to a parking area above a bridge across the Cle Elum River, elevation 2550 feet. (Logging may soon obliterate this trailhead, in which case the trail will be relocated to start from the Waptus River trail [Hike 67], adding about 2 round-trip miles.)

The trail starts by crossing the bridge, goes about ¼ mile, then comes out on a logging road on private property. Follow the road straight ahead, watching closely for the trail on the left. After leaving the logging road, the way is through forest a full mile, in the course of which it reenters National Forest and commences relentless switchbacks due north up the mountainside. Around the 2-mile mark the trees thin, allowing views east and south.

A section of private land is reached about 2½ miles; the trail zigzags over it, traverses the valley head, leaves private property, and then, still with switchbacks, ascends to the old lookout site.

Views are unlimited over the Salmon la Sac area, the Wenatchee

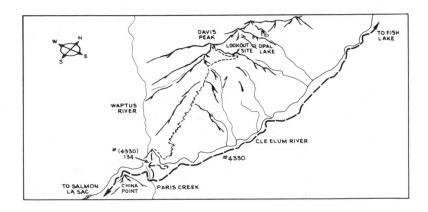

Opal Lake from Davis Peak

Mountains, the Cle Elum valley, and mountains, mountains, mountains. The crest of Davis Peak is shaped like the shoe of a westward-running horse, the lookout on one of the heel tips and Opal Lake on the other. A trail goes west along the edge of the cliffs to the true summit, West Point, at the "toe" of the horseshoe, from which the view is across Waptus Lake to Dutch Miller Gap, 10 crow-miles away.

71 SCATTER CREEK PASS— PADDY-GO-EASY PASS LOOP

Round trip to Scatter Creek Pass
  9 miles
Hiking time 6 hours
High point 6200 feet
Elevation gain 2880 feet
Hikable mid-July through
  September

One day
USGS The Cradle and
  Chiwaukum Mountains

Loop trip 23 miles
Allow 2–3 days
Elevation gain 4800 feet

The two passes have meadows and views, one has a small lake, and both may have people. Between them, though, is just about guaranteed solitude, miles and miles of it along streams through forests, rewarding hikers who do them in a loop rather than separately.

Due to route-finding problems (including the fact that the usually accurate USGS and Forest Service maps show the trail where it isn't) it's best to start on the Scatter Creek end.

Drive to Salmon la Sac (Hike 65) and continue 9 miles on road No. 4330 to Scatter Creek Crossing (the creek is underground most of the summer). Find Scatter Creek trail No. 1328, signed "County Line Trail 2 miles." Elevation, 3320 feet.

Obscure at the start, the trail soon becomes evident as it ascends with virtually no switchbacks 1500 feet to a junction. Go left over Scatter Creek, the trail again evasive and easily lost in sheep-trampled meadows. Several campsites are passed—delightful if the sheep haven't been there lately—as the way generally follows the creek upward to Scatter Creek Pass at 6200 feet, 4½ miles. (Some maps call it "Fish Eagle Pass" but the Forest Service says that's someplace else.) If returning this

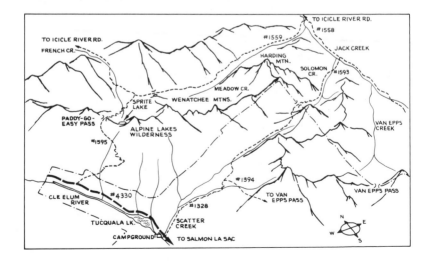

Jack Creek valley from Scatter Creek Pass

way, make careful note of where the creek was crossed; miss that spot and you may be in trouble.

Obvious trail switchbacks down Solomon Creek to Jack Creek trail No. 1558, 8 miles, 4000 feet. Go downstream through forest 2½ miles to a junction, 10½ miles, 3800 feet. Turn left on Meadow Creek trail No. 1559, which climbs gently (mostly) 4½ miles to a wooded pass at 5400 feet and drops 1 mile in French Creek drainage to the junction, 16 miles, 4750 feet, with Paddy-Go-Easy Pass– French Creek trail No 1595. Go left, zigzagging up 1400 feet in 2 miles to Paddy-Go-Easy Pass, 6950 feet. Here you may encounter the first other hikers of the trip. Views are fine out to Mt. Daniel. Flowers bloom in mid-July, even though Sprite Lake, nestled in a small cirque, may be frozen until August. No firewood remains at the lake. Thanks (no thanks) to the archaic 1872 Mining Laws, both the pass and the lake are private land, a good reason to abolish the rotten old law.

From the pass drop 2700 feet in 3 miles to the Cle Elum River road and walk 2 miles on the road past Tucquala (Fish) Lake to Scatter Creek (Hike 72).

Cle Elum River road   Old: 2405
                                     New: 4330

72 PADDY-GO-EASY PASS

Round trip to pass 6 miles
Hiking time 4 hours
High point 6100 feet
Elevation gain 2700 feet

Hikable mid-July through
   September
One day or backpack
USGS The Cradle

A short, steep climb to a high pass with views out to great peaks and down to Fish Lake (Tucquala Lake) and the marshy valley of the Cle Elum River, and then an easy meadow-roaming walk to a lovely little

Sprite Lake

lake. Flowers bloom here in mid-July but the lake is generally frozen until the end of the month.

Drive to Salmon la Sac (Hike 65) and continue 11 miles on road No. 4330, to about .7 mile past Fish Lake Guard Station, and find the trailhead, elevation 3400 feet, on the right side of the road behind a group of tumble-down private cabins along a stream.

Paddy-Go-Easy Pass trail No. 1595 starts in woods and in ½ mile passes a creek, the last water for 2 miles. At 1 mile is a junction with an abandoned trail going to the guard station; keep left. The way now steepens, switchbacking up through dense timber to small meadows with views to the valley and to Cathedral Rock and Mt. Daniel. At about 2½ miles the trail forks (unmarked). The left fork switchbacks directly to the pass. The right fork detours by an old mine and a stream, rejoining the main trail ¼ mile below the pass. The final stretch traverses under red cliffs of a 6500-foot peak to Paddy-Go-Easy Pass, 3½ miles, 6100 feet.

The east slopes of the pass are mostly meadowland. Contour south along the ridge ¼ mile to a point directly above 5900-foot Sprite Lake and descend to the shores. Delightful campsites but no wood, so carry a stove. The tiny lake provides a striking foreground for The Cradle, the impressive 7467-foot peak across the valley.

Cle Elum River road   Old: 2404
                             New: 4330

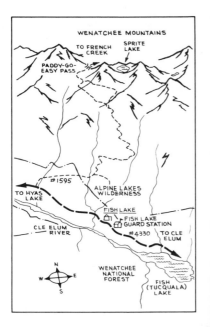

73 CATHEDRAL ROCK– DECEPTION PASS LOOP

Loop trip 14 miles	Hikable July through September
Allow 2–4 days	USGS Mt. Daniel and The Cradle
High point 5500 feet	
Elevation gain 2300 feet	

The basic ramble up and around the terminus of the old Cle Elum Glacier trough, in meadows and by waterfalls and tarns, amid spectacularities of the Alpine Lakes Wilderness, can be done in a couple of easy days. However, two or three more should be allowed for sidetrips to some of the region's most heart-stopping scenery.

Drive to Salmon la Sac (Hike 65) and continue 12.5 miles on road No. 4330 to the end at Hyas Lake–Deception Pass trailhead, elevation 3350 feet.

From the parking area walk the road back a short bit to the last Y, go west a similar distance to the start of Cathedral Rock trail No. 1345, and follow it to Cathedral Pass, 4½ miles, 5500 feet (Hike 75). On the way, at 2½ miles, 4841 feet, is Squaw Lake, the last good camp anywhere in the vicinity that has year-round water. From the intersection at Cathedral Pass the Pacific Crest Trail drops left to Deep Lake, the first of the possible sidetrips, and goes right to Deception Pass.

The 4½ miles of the Crest Trail between the two passes is scenery all the way, views from the alpine gardens across the ground-down-at-the-heel llacial trough and the characteristic marshy lakes, Hyas and Fish, up to the long and blocky ridge of Granite Mountain. At places the Crest Freeway was dynamited, at enormous expense, in cliffs plunging from the summit of Cathedral Rock and spur ridges of Mt. Daniel. (**Note:** The trail has two stream crossings that in the high water of snowmelt season or cloudbursts are formidable to the point of suicidal. Many a party has been forced to turn back and make a long detour via the Cle Elum valley floor; when in doubt, call the Forest Service before setting out.)

At 9 miles from the road the loop reaches Deception Pass, 4475 feet,

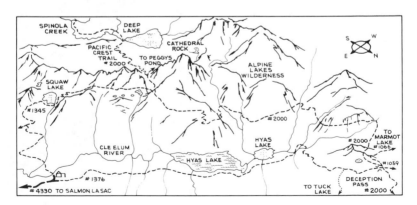

Cathedral Rock and the two Hyas Lakes

and intersects the Marmot Lake trail, the second good sidetrip (Hike 76). Camps near the pass lack water after the snowmelt dries up, but a year-round creek is located ½ mile down the Hyas Lake trail, near the takeoff of the Tuck and Robin Lakes trail, the third recommended sidetrip (Hike 74).

The loop is completed with a quick descent to the floor of the trough and a passage along the shore of Hyas Lake to the road-end, finishing off the last of the 14 miles.

74 TUCK AND ROBIN LAKES

Round trip to Robin Lakes 14 miles
Allow 3–4 days
High point 6250 feet
Elevation gain 3200 feet

Hikable August through mid-October
USGS Mt. Daniel and The Cradle

The "Little Enchantments," they've been called, for the glory of lakes, splendor of granite, deliriums of meadow nooks and broad views—and what often seems the largest alpine population this side of the winter Olympics. The Forest Service tried to hold down use by not building a real trail. We cooperated by removing the trip from a previous edition of this guidebook. But a hiker returns starry-eyed and gasping, friends pry the secret out of him, and there goes the neighborhood. The new management goal is not to hide the place but keep it from being pounded and burned and polluted to death.

Drive from Salmon la Sac to the Hyas Lake–Deception Pass trailhead, elevation 3350 feet (Hike 73).

Walk the valley trail to Hyas Lake at 1½ miles, 3448 feet. The mile-long lake ringed by forest and reedy marsh, dominated by the tower of 6724-foot Cathedral Rock, has many pleasant camps and is popular among novices trying out new gear and families trying out new kids. Beyond the lake, at a scant 4 miles, the trail turns steeply up, switchbacking. At some 4½ miles, 4300 feet, while still a long ½ mile from Deception Pass, the way gentles. Watch for an arrow and an "X" carved in a tree and a trail sign.

An ancient fireman's track, unbuilt, unmaintained, dips to cross two small creeks, bumps against the forest wall, and begins a fascinating alternation of contours to get over or under cliffs and straight-up scrambles to get through them.

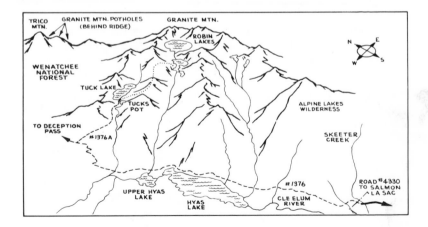

Robin Lake and Mount Daniel

A short bit past a rock promontory in an old burn (stunning views) at 6 miles, 5628 feet, the path levels out to Tuck Lake, surrounded by cliffs. Every square foot of flat ground is an "established camp"—and is in the middle of a path to somewhere—and on a fine weekend is occupied. Except for the small area in the woods where the trail first touches the lake, firewood is zero, and that's good because fires are not permitted. For peaceful and neat camping you'll do better in a zoo.

From the lake outlet take any of the paths along the divider ridge and when it leaps upward ascend to the crest at 5800 feet. Cairns and tread lead along the crest, down and up the side of the ridge to its merger into the mountainside at 6000 feet, then up heather and slabs to a 6250-foot shoulder, and at 1 mile from Tuck, down to Lower Robin Lake, 6163 feet, which connects to Upper Robin, 6178 feet.

Roam as you please in the wide-open parkland. With USGS map in hand, go either way around Upper Robin to easily ascend 7144-foot Granite Mountain. Ramble the up-and-down ridge to 6650-foot Trico Mountain. Gaze down upon and/or prowl around nearly two dozen lakes.

Now, the reason we put the trip back in the book: the sermon. What's good for the Enchantments (Hike 22) is good for the Robins—and maybe not good enough, the area being smaller and more easily accessible. Campers absolutely *must not* initiate new patches of bare dirt or heaps of charcoal. Camp on established patches of dirt. Wood fires are banned; carry a stove. Do not camp in the middle of the zoo—find privacy in countless nooks on ridges or in adjacent basins. We further have suggested to the Forest Service that (1) privies be strategically located; (2) a "day use only" zone be established on the Snow Lake pattern (Hike 84); and (3) the lakes be allowed to be fished out and go barren.

75

DEEP LAKE

Round trip 14½ miles
Hiking time 9 hours
High point 5500 feet
**Elevation gain 2150 feet in, 1200
 feet out**

Hikable July through October
One day or backpack
USGS Mt. Daniel and The Cradle

Climb in forest to beautiful meadow country at the base of Cathedral
Rock. Look in one direction down to the Cle Elum River and beyond to
Mt. Stuart, highest summit in the Alpine Lakes Wilderness, and in the
other to 7960-foot Mt. Daniel, highest summit in King County and the
western section of the Alpine Lakes. Look below to the green valley of
Spinola Creek and, at its head, under the slopes of Daniel, the blue waters of Deep Lake.

Drive to Salmon la Sac (Hike 65) and continue 12.5 miles on road No.
4330 to a Y a short bit from the road-end. The right spur goes a few dozen
yards to the Hyas Lake–Deception Pass trailhead. Take the left spur a
similar distance to the Deep Lake trailhead, elevation 3350 feet.

Cathedral Rock trail No. 1345 (the official moniker) crosses the Cle
Elum River on a bridge and ascends steadily but moderately in cool
forest, at 2 miles passing a junction with Trail Creek trail No. 1322. At
2½ miles the new trail emerges into marshy meadows around the shores
of little Squaw Lake, 4841 feet, a pleasant picnic spot and a good turnaround for an easy afternoon.

The way continues up in alpine forest and patches of flowers and growing views, traverses heather gardens along the ridge slopes, and at 4½
miles, 5500 feet, reaches Cathedral Pass nearly at the foot of Cathedral

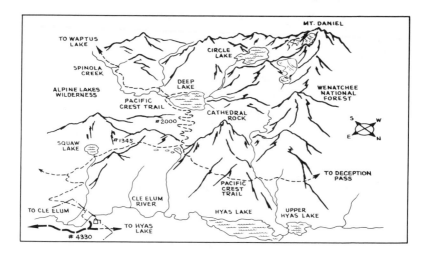

Spinola Creek and shoulder of Mount Daniel

Rock, at this point intersecting the new Pacific Crest Trail coming from Deception Pass.

To descend or not to descend—that is the question. The views from the saddle make it a satisfying destination, and parkland on the crest of the ridge invites wandering; in early summer, snowmelt ponds permit delightful camps.

If the lake is chosen, descend 1200 feet on the Crest Trail, which drops into forest in a long series of switchbacks, at 7¼ miles from your trailhead arriving on the east side of Deep Lake, 4382 feet. Campsites here and elsewhere along the shores. If time allows, explore to broad meadows at the lake outlet and to flowers and waterfalls at the inlet.

The Crest Trail proceeds down Spinola Creek to the Waptus River.

Cle Elum River road   Old: 2405
                       New: 4330

76   MARMOT LAKE

Round trip 17 miles
Allow 2 days
High point 4930 feet
Elevation gain 2400 feet

Hikable July through September
USGS Mt. Daniel and The Cradle

Sample the variety of the Alpine Lakes: Begin with a close-to-the-road and extremely popular valley lake, climb to a cirque lake ringed by cliffs and talus parkland and fishermen, and wander on to a lonesome lake colored jade green by meltwater from a small glacier. Go from forests to heather meadows to moraines. Look up at the peaks from below, then out to the peaks from high viewpoints.

Drive from Salmon la Sac to the Hyas Lake–Deception Pass trailhead, elevation 3350 feet (Hike 73). Hike to Hyas Lake at 1½ miles, 3448 feet. The occupants of most of the scores of cars typically parked at the road-end stop here, content with the wading, swimming, fishing, camping, and scenery-watching.

Continue past the lake and along the river bottom, then up switchbacks with views back down to Hyas Lake and across the valley to Mt. Daniel and Mt. Hinman. At 5 miles the trail tops 4475-foot Deception Pass and intersects the Pacific Crest Trail. Turn left from it on trial No. 1066, signed "Marmot Lake, 3½ miles."

The path ascends gently in parkland, by small ponds (camps), crosses a 4760-foot swale in Blue Ridge, and wends down through the meadow basin of Hozzbizz Lake, 4520 feet, beneath scenic cliffs and waterfalls of Peak 6556. The camps here tend to be horsey but several nice sites are in the woods a short way down Hozzbizz Creek. The trail drops to 3840 feet and resumes climbing, crossing a nameless creek from Marmot Lake and

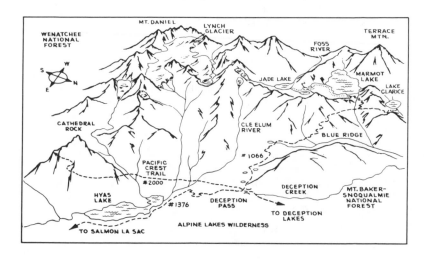

Air view of Marmot Lake, Mount Daniel (left)*, and Mount Hinman* (right)

at 3 miles from Deception Pass coming to a Y. The right fork leads 1 mile to Lake Clarice, 4530 feet. Switchback left, climbing in a final ½ mile to Marmot Lake, 4930 feet, 8½ miles. The best camps (usually horsey, fishy, and garbagey) lie ¼ mile south along the shore. Until the Forest Service installs privies, watch where you throw down your sleeping bag.

The lake is pleasant to gaze upon, its broad waters mirroring Terrace Mountain, but due to cliffs isn't much for easy exploration. If feeling doughty, carry on. A rough, tricky, awkward path goes up and down around Marmot Lake to the inlet and leads steeply and treacherously up a rocky gully, at a long, slow 1 mile leveling out in the meadow draw of No Name Lake, 5600 feet. A few steps more and—wow!—a bit below, at 5442 feet, lies the miracle of Jade Lake, colored by rock milk from the little Jade Glacier between 7250-foot Lynch Peak on the left and 7960-foot Diptop Peak on the right. A path drops to the lake but to proceed to the far shore and upward on the peaks entails travel beyond what the ordinary hiker should try.

Deception Pass and Marmot Lake also can be approached from the north via Deception Creek or Surprise Lake (Hikes 8 and 9).

Yakima River

77 YAKIMA RIM SKYLINE TRAIL

One-way trip 18 miles
Allow 2 days
High point 3630 feet
Elevation gain 1900 feet

Hikable March through May and
in October
One day or backpack
USGS Ellensburg, Badger Pocket,
West Yakima

One term for the great long nakedness of Umptanum Ridge is "big sky country," the constant, uninterrupted views extending east beyond the deep cleft of the Yakima Canyon to the Columbia Plateau, west to the Stuart Range and volcanoes from Rainier to Adams to Hood. "Desert−alpine" is another, expressing the hiker's surprise to find yellow bells, glacier lilies, and shooting stars blooming in draws where the snow has only just melted, while on adjacent sunbaked and rocky slopes the balsamroot and phlox are yellowing and white-splashing whole acres. Coyotes lope through the purple sage, shy rattlesnakes hide in the spring-fed lushness of speedwell and monkeyflower, golden eagles and falcons ride the thermals on the hunt for wee timorous beasties.

Among the lavish display of wildflowers, the procession beginning in March and not burning out until July, are onion and camas and brodiaea and iris, paintbrush and buckwheat and rose and locoweed, lupine and penstemon and desert parsley and wallflower, rabbitbrush and bitterbrush and peppergrass. Perhaps most stunning is the lovely pink bitterroot, and most startling is the near-simultaneous blossoming of both species of cactus native to Washington. Equally rich is the birdlife, climaxing in the hours after dawn at the "Birdsong Tree," a giant locust at The Spring, site of an old homestead on Rosa Creek.

Hikers from the "wet" side of the Cascades are likely to become semi-hysterical amid the unfamiliar richness of color—and the unaccustomed

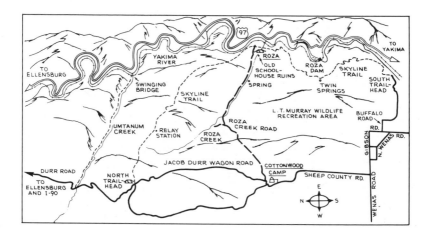

brightness of the sun and the total lack of meaningful forests. Since even in spring the thermometer can top 100 degrees by noon, the typical plan is to start early, at midday look for a patch of aspens or cottonwoods to shade a siesta, and carry a gallon of water per day per hiker. (Contrarily, at these elevations sudden snow squalls can blow in until June and after September.)

Three accesses permit the route to be done on day trips or divided in a two-part backpack or otherwise varied. Directions below are given from north to south, for an elevation gain of 1900 feet, compared to 3700 feet the other way. However, the road to the North and Rosa trailheads is bad and getting worse. And until funds are available for improvements, expect it to remain that way. When conditions are too ominous for the favorite family BMW to comfortably cruise to the North or Rosa trailheads, head for the South trailhead on well-maintained roads.

North trailhead: At Ellensburg leave Interstate 90 on Exit 109 and take a right, driving Canyon Road north .6 mile toward town. Go off left on Damman Road, which becomes Umptanum Road. In 5.4 miles is an intersection with Durr Road, a restored wagon road; go left 7.1 miles to the trailhead, elevation 3100 feet. (Trailhead, located by a large information board, was not signed in 1985.)

Rosa Creek trailhead: From the North trailhead continue south on Durr Road 5.6 miles to Rosa Creek Road; turn left for 6.1 miles to Rosa Camp, 1300 feet. While descending the valley of Rosa Creek, note a lush green patch by the road; "The Spring" is the only reliable water between the North trailhead and here. A party camped at the old homestead site can ascend open sagebrush slopes to the ridge, there intersecting the trail (though in this country no trail is really needed).

South trailhead: Continue south on Durr Road, which near the exit of L. T. Murray Wildlife Recreation Area changes name to Sheep County Road. Intersect Wenas Road and turn left on it 1.8 miles to Gibson Road; go right .3 mile to Buffalo Road; go left .5 mile to an L. T. Murray sign; go right the final 2.4 miles to the trailhead, 1300 feet. When the South trailhead is the destination, leave Interstate 90 on Exit 109 and take a right, south, on Canyon Road, Highway 821, for 28.7 miles along the Yakima River to the Selah exit. Go right 1.9 miles on Harrison Road, then right again on Wenas Road for 3.1 miles to meet Gibson Road opposite the fire station. Continue on as noted above to Buffalo and the trailhead.

From the North trailhead an old wagon road follows the crest of the broad-backed basalt ridge, overlooking the steep-walled Umptanum Creek Canyon. Tempting and possibly confusing unsigned roads and trails radiate out in various directions from the main trail. Stick to the ridge crest; in this open country it is hard to get lost. The way gains only 500 feet in the first 1¾ rolling miles to an abandoned microwave relay station, views ranging from excellent to exceptional.

At 4 miles the trail leaves the old road and begins a long descent along the ridge crest, starting easy and steepening, at 9 miles reaching Rosa Camp, next to the foundation of the old schoolhouse. Numerous other signs of the vanished settlement are seen during the 2-mile walk up Rosa Creek Road to The Spring, either to fetch water or to camp.

Sunflowers

From Rosa Camp the trail climbs to the 3000-foot high point of the south half of the route, then descends gently to Twin Springs, 2800 feet, the shade and water appreciated by hikers and wildlife. A short ascent returns to a high rim overlooking the Yakima River, more than 2000 feet directly below. The way proceeds along the rim in flowers and birds and views, at last dropping to the South trailhead at 18 miles.

Another 8 miles can be added to the route by starting from the Canyon Road (the old Ellensburg-Yakima Highway 821), crossing the Yakima River on the swinging bridge, walking the Umptanum Creek trail 4 miles to the recreation site, and then Durr Road 4 miles to the North trailhead. (The Umptanum Creek trail also is a superb day walk from Canyon Road, especially in early spring when the Umptanum-Durr Roads may be passable only by four-wheel drive.)

78 JOHN WAYNE PIONEER TRAIL

Round trip 15 miles
Hiking time 7 hours
High point 1840 feet
Elevation loss 120 feet

Hikable March through
  mid-November
One day (camping not presently
  allowed)
USGS Cle Elum and Thorp

When the Milwaukee Road ceased running trains and the tracks were torn up, the west-east line across the State of Washington might quickly have gone into a multiplicity of private ownerships.

Instead, thanks to the alertness of a group of dedicated and diligent horse folk and their sympathizers in the Legislature, the route from Easton to Idaho was obtained by the state and dubbed the John Wayne Pioneer Trail, a route for hiking, riding horses, and driving olden-style covered wagons. The ultimate vision sees the route extended over the Cascades to a western terminus at, perhaps, Issaquah, and eastward through Idaho to—Independence, Missouri?

However, there's many a slip. To date only the 25 miles easterly from Easton are readily accessible to the general public, under administration of state parks. The rest of the trail is under jurisdiction of the state Department of Natural Resources, open to public travel only April 15 to May 31 and in October, and then strictly by paid permit. (Permits are available from Milwaukee Road Specialist, Department of Natural Resources Southeast Area, 713 Bowers Road, Ellensburg 98926). The DNR lacks the manpower and funds to preserve the trail, which currently is being illegally preempted for private uses by adjoining property owners who vow to get the trail eliminated.

The help of hikers will be essential if wagon trails are to continue to roll, as they do now despite man-made difficulties, offering all Americans the opportunity for a unique outdoor experience, a re-creation of the days and ways of the pioneers. The 25 state park miles start in Easton and traverse farm and cattle country of the Yakima Valley, crossing the Yakima River twice on airy bridges. The best introductory sampling for the hiker is the final 7 miles, ending at a tunnel in a narrow gorge where the Yakima River sinuously winds between steep, rocky, sagebrush slopes.

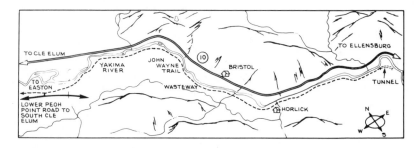

Yakima River

Drive Interstate 90 east 22 miles from Snoqualmie Pass, take Exit 84, and drive toward Cle Elum .7 mile. As the road descends into town take a right, following signs to Swiftwater Trailer Park. In .3 mile the road passes under the freeway, crosses the Yakima River, enters South Cle Elum, and becomes 4th Street. Bear left, uphill, .6 mile to an intersection. Take a left on Lower Peoh Point Road. In 2.2 miles pass under the freeway again and at .6 mile beyond find the trail access and parking on the left side of the road, elevation 1840 feet.

The rail grade, sans rails and ties, is in excellent condition and walking is easy. Pass a small barn and adjacent cows and parallel the Yakima River, enjoying views of the Stuart Range. After ½ mile the trail shortcuts a bend in the river, returning to it in ½ mile, just in time to admire its confluence with the Teanaway River. At a broad bend the trail again wanders away from the river, tunnels through a friendly grove of trees, returns to the river, and at 2½ miles passes a broad swath of buzzing power lines. Ahead the valley opens into Bristol Flat, an isolated farmland flat boxed in by steep, dry hills, flower-bright in early spring (as is the whole trail route). Continuing straight and nearly level, the way goes by a large overflow from an irrigation canal on the hill above and at 4½ miles passes the old town of Horlick.

The river now bends east, the valley narrows, and the walls rise steeply. Highway 10 for the first time climbs above the trail. The scenery becomes dramatic as the grade cuts canyon walls a few feet above the powerful surge of the Yakima River. At 7½ miles the canyon walls close in and the river makes a sharp bend around a particularly massive outcropping of basalt which the railroad tunneled straight through. The section beyond is open only by permit.

Remember: Bring your flower book and your birding binoculars. Watch for snakes, which are harmless unless you frighten them. Carry a gallon of water per person.

79 RACHEL LAKE– RAMPART RIDGE

Round trip to Rachel Lake 8 miles
Hiking time 6 hours
High point 4700 feet
Elevation gain 1900 feet
Hikable mid-July through
October
One day or backpack
USGS Snoqualmie Pass

Round trip to Rampart Lakes 11
miles
Hiking time 8 hours
High point 5200 feet
Elevation gain 2400 feet

A cool and green valley forest, a large alpine lake walled by glacier-carved cliffs that drop straight to the water, a heaven of rock-bowl lakelets and ponds, gardens of heather and blossoms, and ridges and nooks for prowling. On summer weekends hundreds of hikers throng Rachel Lake and dozens are in every pocket and on every knob of the high ridge, where hikers have woven a spiderweb of paths.

The trail, posted "hikers only," was never built but simply beaten into existence by thousands of feet. The way goes around, up, or down to avoid obstacles and hardly knows how to switchback. But bad is good—if the route were built to freeway standards the highland would be visited not by regiments but swarming hordes.

Drive Interstate 90 east from Snoqualmie Pass 12.5 miles, take Lake Kachess Exit 62, and follow signs 5 miles to Kachess Lake Campground. Turn left 4 miles on Box Canyon road No. 4930 to a junction. Turn left .2 mile and hope to find space for your car in the enormous parking lot at the Rachel Lake trailhead, elevation 2800 feet.

The hike begins with a mile of moderate ascent to a rest stop by water-carved and pot-holed and moss-carpeted slabs. The trail levels out along the creek for 1½ miles. In an open swath of avalanche greenery, look up to 6032-foot Hi Box Mountain. At 2½ miles the valley ends in an abrupt headwall and rough tread proceeds straight up, rarely bothering to switchback, gaining 1300 feet in a cruel mile, suffering alleviated by glories of cool-breeze rest-stop waterfalls. Suddenly the angle eases and

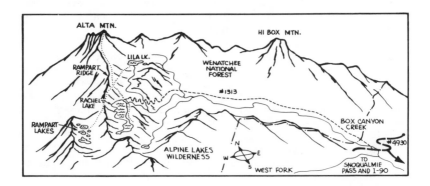

Lila Lake and Hibox Mountain

forest yields to meadows and at 4 miles, 4700 feet, is Rachel Lake.

Follow paths around the lake, admiring blue waters ringed by trees and cliffs—and numerous campsites. Go left past the narrows to the secluded south bay.

To visit higher country, do not circle the lake but turn right at the shore on a boot-built path climbing above the cirque, with views down to the lake and out Box Canyon Creek. After a steep ½ mile the trail flattens in a wide parkland saddle, 5200 feet, and reaches an unmarked junction offering a choice.

Go right 1 mile to 5200-foot Lila Lake (actually *two* lakes, or maybe six, plus ponds, scattered about a variegated basin) or walk a meadow tightrope in the sky to (or near) the summit of 6240-foot Alta Mountain.

Go left an up-and-down mile to 5100-foot Rampart Lakes. Examine in detail each of the little lakes and tiny ponds, the surrounding buttresses, waterfalls, and peaceful mountain homes. Note the mixture of basalts, conglomerates, and rusty mineralized lobes. Snoop into a flowery corner, climb a heather knoll, think about roaming the short but rough way south to Lake Lillian (Hike 81), and before you know it, arrive on the crest of 5800-foot Rampart Ridge and enjoy views down to Gold Creek, west to Snoqualmie Pass, south to Rainier and Adams, east to Stuart, and north to Three Queens and Chimney Rock.

Camping . . . This is one of those areas where popularity is forcing out waterside camps, wood fires, dogs, horses, and fish, leaving only the incomparable alpine wildland beauty.

Box Canyon road   Old: 2214
                  New: 4930

GOLD CREEK

Round trip to Alaska Lake 11½ miles
Hiking time 9 hours
High point 4200 feet
Elevation gain 1600 feet
Hikable mid-July through September

One day or backpack
USGS Snoqualmie Pass

Round trip to Joe Lake 14 miles
Hiking time 9 hours
High point 4624 feet
Elevation gain 2000 feet

Miles of rushing streams, tall trees, vine maple, and slide alder under the steep walls of Rampart Ridge to the east and equally steep cliffs of Kendall Peak to the west. Then rugged paths to either of two beautiful alpine lakes– and views– and highland roaming– and access to one of the more spectacular sections of the Pacific Crest Trail, the Katwalk.

When early-summer snow lingers on the Katwalk (Hike 82) or early fall snow makes the Pacific Crest Trail too dangerous to hike, the alternative to steep, slippery, and exposed cliffs is to ascend or descend Gold Creek via Joe Lake.

For years this trail was abandoned by the Forest Service and eventually, as the blowdowns to be crawled over or wiggled under numbered well over a hundred, by hikers as well. When the Pacific Crest Trail was rerouted to traverse the head of Gold Creek the path was forgotten altogether. However, thanks to very ambitious volunteers, by 1984 the first 4-mile section was cleared out, some signs replaced, and some brush cut from the upper sections.

Drive Interstate 90 east 2 miles from Snoqualmie Pass to Hyak Exit 54. Follow the Forest Service road on the north side of the highway, paralleling the interstate .8 mile. Cross Gold Creek and turn left on road No. 22019. In .5 mile the road branches four ways. Take the second fork from the right and continue about 1 mile, keeping right at most junctions, and avoiding sideroads to recreation homes and one road that

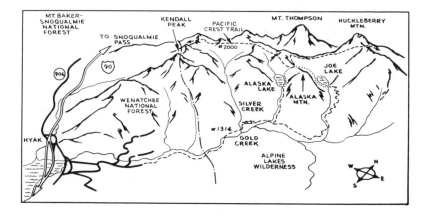

Huckleberry Mountain from Joe Lake

climbs quickly to a clearcut high on the mountain. Park on the roadside at the trailhead, elevation 2600 feet.

The rough trail starts on the east side of the valley, alternating between woods and brush, with one pleasant and easy passage along a gravel bar. Clearcuts can be seen across the river, but soon the limit of logging is reached and the forest scene becomes wild and pure. At about 3 miles cross Gold Creek (on a footlog or by wading) and continue up the west side of the valley, at about 3½ miles crossing Silver Creek. At 3¾ miles is the last of numerous riverside camps. At 4½ miles cross Alaska Creek and ¼ mile beyond, in a tiny, grassy, marshy meadow, find an unmarked junction, 3000 feet. Campsites here, and views to Alta Mountain and Chikamin Ridge and Peak.

The left fork climbs a steep mile up a tributary through vine maple and slide alder and finally a rockslide to 4200-foot Alaska Lake.

The right fork proceeds up the main valley, contouring and climbing through avalanche greenery, then trees, another mile around the base of Alaska Mountain. Now the way turns steeply uphill, gaining 1000 feet in ½ mile, passing two lovely waterfalls on a hazardous staircase of rocks, roots, and trees. Be particularly cautious on the descent—a slip could cause a serious fall. Near the top is a fine view down Gold Creek to Lake Keechelus and Mt. Rainier. At last the route abruptly flattens out for a short, level romp to the shores of 4624-foot Joe Lake, set in an alpine cirque beneath the spire of 6300-foot Huckleberry Mountain and the heather-and-forest slopes of Alaska Mountain. Over the ridge to the west can be seen the tower of 6554-foot Mt. Thompson, and across the valley to the east, the fluted walls of Chikamin Ridge.

Hikers choosing to camp near a lake should climb from Joe Lake to the Pacific Crest Trail and find designated campsites west of Huckleberry Mountain.

MOUNT MARGARET—
LAKE LILLIAN

Round trip to Twin Lakes 6 miles
Hiking time 5 hours
High point 5520 feet
Elevation gain 1500 feet
Hikable late June through
  October
One day
USGS Snoqualmie Pass

Round trip to Lake Lillian 9 miles
Hiking time 6 hours
High point 5200 feet
Elevation gain 1300 feet in, 500
  feet out
Hikable July through September
One day or backpack

A short climb to a little mountain with big views, then onward in meadows to a secluded alpine lake, a fine basecamp for highland roaming on Rampart Ridge.

Drive Interstate 90 east from Snoqualmie Pass 2 miles to Hyak Exit 54 and find the Forest Service road on the north side of the highway. This road parallels the Interstate for 2.5 miles to Rocky Run and then climbs another 1.5 miles, passing several well-marked intersections to a large parking lot, elevation 3800 feet.

Walk the road a few hundred feet farther and take a steep abandoned logging track that eventually turns into a trail and enters forest. The trail climbs, with numerous switchbacks, to the ridge top at 5000 feet, a few hundred feet below the summit of Mt. Margaret. From here the Margaret Lake trail drops over the far side of the ridge and descends to the lake 300 feet below. For a view of forest and three or four small lakes, step a few feet over the crest of the ridge and look down. Besides Margaret, there are Stonethrow, Swan, and Rock Rabbit Lakes.

From the ridge the trail climbs a bit, then contours around the west side of Mt. Margaret. (For more views, scramble to the summit. One place is as good as the next—there's no trail.) On the north side of the mountain the trail descends meadows to shallow Twin Lakes at 3 miles, 4700 feet; the campsites aren't at all bad.

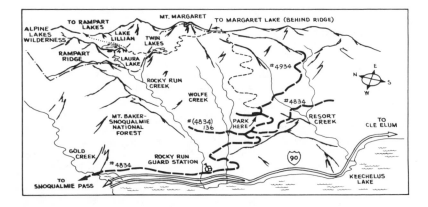

Twin Lake on trail to Lake Lillian

Now the trail becomes more difficult. The tread is rough and at times steep as it loses another 200 feet and then climbs back up 300 feet. At 4½ miles, 4800 feet, is lovely Lake Lillian amid glacier-polished rocks and heather and flowers and alpine trees. The shore slopes are so steep that flat space for sleeping is very scanty.

For wandering, climb from the lake to lonesome little basins or to broad views atop Rampart Ridge.

Old:	2202	2202A	2212
New:	4834	(4834)136	4934

82   KENDALL KATWALK– SPECTACLE POINT

Round trip to Katwalk 10½ miles
Hiking time 7 hours
High point 5400 feet
Elevation gain 2700 feet in, 300 feet out
Hikable mid-July through mid-October
One day
USGS Snoqualmie Pass

Round trip to Spectacle Point 31 miles
Allow 3–4 days
High point 5700 feet
Elevation gain 5500 feet in, 3000 feet out
Hikable mid-July through September

The bag of superlatives is quickly exhausted on this, one of the most spectacular parts of the Cascade section of the Pacific Crest Trail, and the most accessible and popular.

Drive Interstate 90 to Exit 52 at Snoqualmie Pass. Go off the freeway

Kendall Peak and The Katwalk

on the Alpental road several hundred feet to the Pacific Crest Trail parking lot, elevation a bit above 3004 feet.

The trail ascends forest 2 miles, loses 250 feet to negotiate a boulder field, and at 2¾ miles passes the Commonwealth Basin trail (Hike 83). Flattening briefly, the way switchbacks endlessly upward, at 4300 feet crosses an all-summer creek that may be the last water until Ridge Lake, and at 4700 feet attains the wooded crest at Kendall Ridge. On a long traverse around the mountain the path opens out in Kendall Gardens, the start of alpine color that is virtually continuous to Spectacle Point. At 5¼ miles, on a 5400-foot bump, is a happy turnaround for a day hike.

To continue involves stepping carefully along the Kendall Katwalk, blasted across a cliff in solid granite. When snowfree it's safe enough. When snowy, forget it. The mountainside moderates to heather meadows. At 6¼ miles is the 5270-foot saddle between tiny Ridge Lake and large Gravel Lake, the last trail camp until Mineral Creek Park.

Overnighters based here typically daytrip to Alaska Mountain, 7¾ miles, 5745 feet, or to Huckleberry-Chikamin saddle, 10¼ miles, 5520 feet (due to ups and downs, a gross elevation gain of 1100 feet from Ridge Lake). On the way the trail swings around the basins of Alaska Lake and Joe Lake, both 1000 feet below and without recommendable sidetrails. The saddle is a precinct of heaven but is also so fragile that to camp here would be a sin, if not a capital crime.

The upsy-downsy trail swings across the magnificent cliff-and-meadow face of Chikamin Peak and Four Brothers to a pass overlooking Park Lakes, on the Cascade Crest at 5700 feet, 14 miles. The path descends the alpine basin of Mineral Creek Park to an established camp at 5200 feet, 14½ miles, dips farther to a 4970-foot pass near Park Pond and a junction with the Park Lakes trail (Hike 64). A final ascent of benches and swales tops out at 5475 feet, 15½ miles, on a shoulder of Three Queens Mountain. Southward ¼ mile along a meadow vale is an all-year creek that waters the grandest trail camps of the area. Sit on the prow of Spectacle Point jutting out in the sky and watch the sun go down. And come up. Beneath your feet sprawls Spectacle Lake (4350 feet, 2½ miles down the Crest Trail and then a sidetrail; Hike 62). Across the valley Glacier Lake snuggles in a cirque. Above rises the long rough wall of Four Brothers, Chikamin, Lemah, Chimney Rock, and Summit Chief.

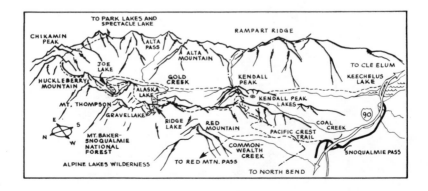

83 COMMONWEALTH BASIN— RED PASS

Round trip to pass 10 miles
Hiking time 5 hours
High point 5400 feet
Elevation gain 2700 feet in, 250 feet out

Hikable mid-July through October
One day or backpack
USGS Snoqualmie Pass

Hikers who have sorrowed for the degradation of Snoqualmie Pass over the past third of a century tend not to go there anymore, because of the pain. However, those diehards who clenched jaws and toughed it out in the legislative battleground saved Commonwealth Basin, the heart of the matter, for wilderness. Here are a peaceful subalpine forest, pure and rippling creeks—an enclave of "olden days" perfect for a family picnic or experimental backpack.

Drive Interstate 90 to Exit 52 at Snoqualmie Pass. Go off the freeway on the Alpental road and within several hundred feet find the Pacific Crest Trail parking lot, elevation something above 3004 feet.

The ancient and honorable trail got to the basin in merely 1 mile, but on private land that ultimately was clearcut, causing the old path to erode so severely it was abandoned. The new way takes 2¾ miles to make the same distance and in the doing gains 700 feet of which 250 are lost. That's progress for you.

Follow the Pacific Crest Trail (Hike 82) 2¾ miles, to where it dips near

Blueberries

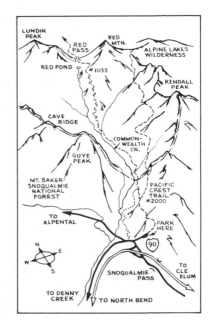

Picking blueberries at Red Pass; Mount Thompson, center

the valley floor before starting up Kendall Peak. A signed sidepath, trail No. 1033, drops to the old Commonwealth Basin trail. Go left or right or straight ahead off the trail for picnics—or for camps to try out brand-new gear, or new kids.

The basin trail turns upstream 1 mile to the valley head and ascends the crest of an open-forested spur in many, many short switchbacks. At last the way flattens out in heather gardens and alpine trees of a cirque basin at the foot of Red Mountain. A few steps away on a sidetrail is Red Pond, 4½ miles, 4900 feet. Eat lunch, tour the bouldery and flowery shores, listen for marmots whistling, walk to the edge of the cirque and look over the valley and the rimming peaks and south to Mt. Rainier. Campsites are overused but pleasant; carry a stove and don't hack the shrubbery.

The trail swings up talus and rock buttresses almost but not quite to the saddle and follows the ridge west to Red Pass, 5 miles, 5400 feet, and views to the deep Middle Fork Snoqualmie valley, the sharp tower of Mt. Thompson, the rugged Chimney Rock group and far horizons.

This used to be the official Cascade Crest Trail and descended from the pass to the Middle Fork Snoqualmie River trail (Hike 94); a doughty soul can do it yet.

SNOW LAKE–GEM LAKE

Round trip to Snow Lake 8 miles
Hiking time 6 hours
High point 4400 feet
Elevation gain 1300 feet in, 400
  feet out

Hikable July through October
One day or backpack
USGS Snoqualmie Pass and
  Bandera

Snow Lake, the largest alpine lake (more than a mile long) near Snoqualmie Pass. On one side cliffs rise steeply to Chair Peak, and on the other forests fall steeply toward the broad, deep gulf of the Middle Fork Snoqualmie River. The trail and lake are overwhelmingly popular—some 14,000 visitors a year, 500 and more on a fine summer Sunday. If it's the sound of silence you're seeking, be warned.

Drive Interstate 90 to Exit 52 at Snoqualmie Pass and go left 2 miles on the Alpental road through the ski area and subdivision to the parking lot and trailhead, elevation 3100 feet.

The trail cimbs a bit in forest to intersect the generations-old hiking route from the pass, obliterated by the Alpental subdividers, and ascends gradually, sometimes in cool trees, sometimes on open slopes with looks over the 3800-foot droplet of Source Lake (the source of the South Fork Snoqualmie River) to Denny Mountain, now civilized, and to The Tooth and Chair Peak, still wild.

The way swings around the valley head and switchbacks a steep ½ mile in heather and flowers and parkland to the saddle, 3½ miles, 4400 feet, between Source Creek and Snow Lake. Not until here is the Alpine Lakes Wilderness entered. Day hikers may well be content with the picnic spots in blossoms and blueberries and splendid views. The trail drops sharply ½ mile from the saddle to meadow shores of Snow Lake, 4 miles, 4016 feet, and rounds the north side.

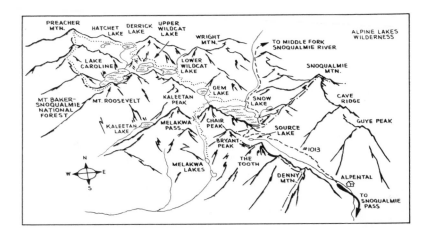

Gem Lake

Now, about the camping. To provide the highest possible quality of experience without limiting the number of visitors, the Forest Service has devised a management plan for Snow Lake—a plan that informs hikers about "The Responsibility of Freedom." Within a "day use area" along the shore first reached by trail, hikers are asked not to camp. In the adjoining "heavy use area," camping should be at established sites only and with no wood fires; carry a stove. So you want to camp free and lonesome? Well, all around the basin, away from the lake, are private nooks. Get off the trail. Snoop around. Learn how to hide.

More lakes, more private, lie beyond. Walk the shore ½ mile to where the Rock Creek trail (Hike 95) comes up from the Middle Fork valley and a bit beyond to the creek, which is the lake's outlet. Hereabouts is a confusion of paths, most beaten out by wandering hikers and dead-ending at cliffs. To solve the puzzle turn lakeward, find where the lakeside trail makes a single switchback down to the outlet, and cross on a logjam. The way leaves the Alpine Lakes Wilderness high above Snow Lake and in 1 mile from the outlet reaches Gem lake, 4800 feet, and several camps.

You wish for still more? The path circles the east shore, climbs a 5000-foot pass, and drops 1000 feet to the two Wildcat Lakes.

85   DENNY CREEK– MELAKWA LAKE

Round trip to Melakwa outlet 9 miles
Hiking time 6 hours
High point 4600 feet
Elevation gain 2300 feet

Hikable mid-July through October
One day or backpack
USGS Snoqualmie Pass

The liveliest valley of the Snoqualmie Pass vicinity, a series of waterfalls fluming and splashing. Beyond is the most spectacular alpine scenery, with snowfields and cliffs of Kaleetan, Chair, and Bryant Peaks rising above the little lake, one shore in forest, the other in rocks and flowers.

Drive Interstate 90 to Exit 47. Go off on the Denny Creek road, turn right, and continue 3 miles to Denny Creek Campground. Just past it turn left on a road over the river and follow it .2 mile, passing private homes, to the road-end parking area and trailhead, elevation 2300 feet.

The trail ascends moderately along Denny Creek in forest, passing under Interstate 90, crossing the stream on a bridge at ½ mile and recrossing at 1 mile, 2800 feet, below water-smoothed slabs of a lovely cataract. The way leaves forest and strikes upward in avalanche greenery to Keekwulee Falls, 1½ miles.

The next ½ mile of tight switchbacks ascends around cliffs past Snowshoe Falls. By this time the majority of Sunday strollers have found precisely the perfect spot for a picnic.

The next comparably rich rewards are a good bit farther on. At 2 miles, 3500 feet, the path flattens out in the upper basin, shortly crosses the creek, goes from trees to low brush to trees again, and switchbacks to wooded Hemlock Pass, 3½ miles, 4600 feet. From here the trail drops a bit in forest to the outlet of Melakwa Lake, 4½ miles, 4550 feet.

Enjoy views of talus, snowfields, and cliffs falling abruptly from the 6200-foot summits of Kaleetan and Chair. The basin is so heavily pounded it's really best not to camp in it at all—at least until a management plan is completed, specifying permitted sites (if any). To avoid dis-

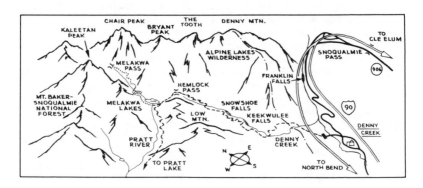

198

Keekwulee Falls

appointment, check with the Forest Service in advance—or come prepared to continue on to camps elsewhere.

For another way back to the highway, and for lonesome walking, take the 3-mile trail from Melakwa Lake to Pratt Lake (Hike 86).

86   PRATT LAKE

Round trip to saddle 11½ miles
Hiking time 8 hours
High point 4100 feet
Elevation gain 2300 feet in, 700
  feet out

Hikable July through October
One day or backpack
USGS Snoqualmie Pass and
  Bandera

Miles of deep forest and a lovely lake amid subalpine trees. A network of trails leads to other lakes and to meadow ridges and high views. From a basecamp hikers and fishermen can spend days exploring.

Drive Interstate 90 to Exit 47, cross over the freeway, and turn west .2 mile to the trailhead parking area, elevation 1800 feet.

The first steep mile gains 800 feet in cool forest to a junction with the Granite Mountain trail; just beyond is a nice creek. Turn left and sidehill upward on a gentler grade in young forest, through patches of twinflower, Canadian dogwood, salal, and bracken, by many nurse logs, to Lookout Point, 3 miles, 3400 feet, a much-used camp.

At 3¾ miles is a short sidepath down to Talapus and Olallie Lakes (Hike 88). The main trail rounds the Olallie basin in open subalpine forest to a 4100-foot saddle, 4 miles, a logical turnaround point for day hikers. Lots of huckleberries here in season, plus a view south to Mt. Rainier, and a junction with the Mt. Defiance trail (see below). The Pratt Lake trail switchbacks down a steep hillside of much mud, some of it covered with new puncheon, flattens out and contours above the lake, then drops to the outlet, 5¾ miles, 3400 feet. The once-popular campsites at the outlet have been mostly destroyed by blowdown. In any event, the lake is so heavily used the Forest Service requests campers to stay elsewhere.

Now, for explorations. (These are only a few; connoisseurs of the coun-

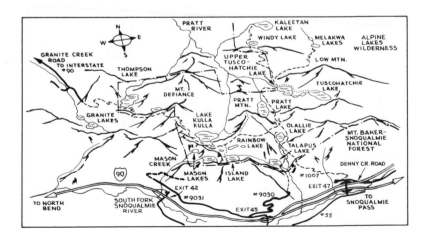

Pratt Lake from Pratt Mountain

try have many other private favorites.)

In a short ½ mile from Pratt Lake is Upper Tuscohatchie Lake, 3400 feet, and a choice of three directions for wandering: A fishermen's path beats brush 1½ miles to Tuscohatchie Lake, 4023 feet. From the outlet of Upper Tuscohatchie a trail ascends gently, then steeply, 3 miles, in trees with glimpses outward of alpine scenery, to 4500-foot Melakwa Lake (Hike 85). Also from the outlet of Upper Tuscohatchie, a less-used trail climbs northward to 4800 feet and drops past little Windy Lake to Kaleetan Lake, 3900 feet, 3½ miles. The way is entirely in forest, with only occasional views over the Pratt River valley, logged in the 1930s, but the lonesome lake has a splendid backdrop in the cliffs of Kaleetan Peak.

From the Olallie-Pratt saddle (see above), the Mt. Defiance trail ascends westward through beargrass and heather and huckleberry meadows (fine views 1100 feet down to Lake Talapus) on the side of Pratt Mountain, whose 5099-foot summit is an easy scramble via huge boulder fields on the southwest side, passes Rainbow Lake (Island Lake lies ½ mile away on a sidepath and actually is a more rewarding objective for hikers than Pratt Lake), comes near Mason Lake, traverses high above Lake Kulla Kulla, and climbs past flower gardens almost to the summit of 5584-foot Defiance, about 3 miles, and broad views (Hike 90). The trail continues westward on the ridge a mile, drops to Thompson Lake, 3400 feet, 5½ miles, and descends to the Granite Creek road, 7 miles.

87 GRANITE MOUNTAIN

Round trip 8 miles
Hiking time 8 hours
High point 5629 feet
Elevation gain 3800 feet

Hikable July through October
One day
USGS Snoqualmie Pass

The most popular summit trail in the Snoqualmie region, and for good reason. Though the ascent is long and in midsummer can be blistering hot, the upper slopes are a delightful garden of granite and flowers, and the panorama includes Mt. Rainier south, Mt. Baker and Glacier Peak north, Chimney Rock and Mt. Stuart east, and infinitely more peaks, valleys, and lakes.

Tragically, this lovely mountain is one of the most notorious killers in the Cascades. In spring its sunny southwest shoulder melts free of snow very early, deceptively seeming to provide bare-trail access to the heights. But the trail doesn't stay on the shoulder; it crosses a gully where snow lingers late and where climax avalanches thunder to the very edge of the freeway, sadly often carrying the bodies of hikers.

Drive Interstate 90 to Exit 47, cross over the freeway, and turn west .5 mile to the trailhead parking lot, elevation 1800 feet.

The first steep mile on the Pratt Lake trail gains 800 feet in cool forest to the Granite Mountain junction and a creek for resting. This may be the last water.

Go right from the 2600-foot junction, traversing in trees ½ mile, then heading straight up and up in countless short switchbacks on an open south slope where fires and avalanches have inhibited the growth of forest. (On sunny days, start early to beat the heat.)

At 4000 feet the trail abruptly gentles and swings east across the avalanche gully—an area of potentially extreme danger perhaps through

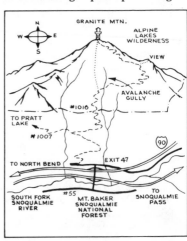

June. Hikers seeking the summit before July should be very wary of crossing this gully; better to be content with the already very nice views to the south over the Snoqualmie valley to Rainier and go home alive.

Beyond the gully the trail sidehills through rock gardens, passing a waterfall (early summer only) from snows above, and then switchbacks steeply to grass and flowers, reaching the summit ridge at 5200 feet. In early summer the route beyond here may be too snowy for some tastes; if so, wander easterly on the crest for splendid views over the Snoqualmie Pass peaks, down to alpine lakes, and through the pass to lake Keechelus.

The trail ascends westward in meadows, above cozy cirque-scoop benches, and switchbacks to the fire lookout, 5629 feet, 4 miles, and full compensation for the struggle.

It is possible to camp near the summit, either for the sunset and dawn views or to allow time for exploration.

The hike has special appeal in early summer when flowers are blooming and in fall when blueberries are ripe and the slopes are flaming.

Mount Rainier and the Granite Mountain trail

Olallie Lake

SOUTH FORK SNOQUALMIE RIVER
Partially in Alpine Lakes Wilderness

TALAPUS LAKE—
OLALLIE LAKE

Round trip to Olallie Lake 4 miles
Hiking time 3 hours
High point 3780 feet
Elevation gain 1220 feet

Hikable June through
   mid-October
One day or backpack
USGS Bandera

A well-groomed forest trail, perfect for first-time backpackers and families with young hikers, leads to two popular lakes with excellent camps and gives access to many more, the area crisscrossed by trails providing infinite opportunity for exploration. Due to the proximity to Puget Sound City, weekenders should arrive early to secure a desirable camp—weekly average of 425 hikers visits here throughout June, July, and August, mostly on weekends.

Drive Interstate 90 to Bandera Airfield Exit 45, go off and under the freeway, then straight ahead west 1 mile on road No. 9030 to a split. Go right, uphill, still on road No. 9030, for 2.4 miles to the end at Talapus Lake trail No. 1039, elevation 2560 feet.

The trail begins on an overgrown logging road through an old clearcut, enters forest shade, and in several gentle switchbacks and a long sidehill swing reaches a marshy area just below Talapus Lake. Paths here branch in several directions. The muddy track that stays on the north side of the lake's outlet stream leads to several secluded camps on the west shore. The driest and best-maintained is the main trail, which crosses the outlet on a bridge and at 1¼ miles comes to Talapus Lake, 3200 feet. Forest camps virtually ring the lake.

The way continues, ascending over a rib ½ mile to meet the sidetrail down from the Pratt Lake trail (Hike 86); turn left ¼ mile to Olallie Lake, 3780 feet, completely wooded, with numerous camps.

To proceed, ascend either by the sidetrail or directly from the far end of Olallie Lake to the Pratt Lake trail. Meadows and views start immediately.

Bandera Viewpoint road   Old: 2218
                                      New: 9030

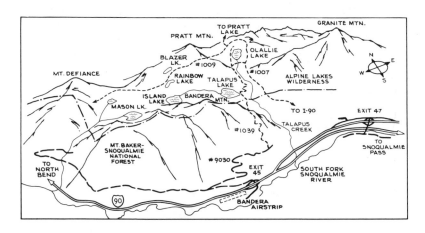

89 MASON LAKE– MOUNT DEFIANCE

Round trip to Mason Lake 5 miles
Hiking time 6 hours
High point 4300 feet
Elevation gain 2200 feet
Hikable June through November
One day or backpack
USGS Bandera

Round trip to Mt. Defiance 10 miles
Hiking time 10 hours
High point 5400 feet
Elevation gain 3300 feet
Hikable July through October

Reasons this hike ought not be in this book at all: a huge and nasty boulder field; a steep, eroded, muddy path—even to call it a "trail" requires a stretch of the imagination. Any person who makes this trip his first hike most likely never will leave the car again. The nearby Lake Annette and Pratt Lake trails are much better suited to beginners and families with small children.

Reasons it's in this book after all: it's one of the closest-to-Seattle trails to a mountain lake; despite the horrors, it's short and on a summer day is thronged with day hikers and dogs, young couples carrying babies on backs, and novices with enormous overnight packs; and to give the devil its due, the alpine lakes are numerous and the views from Mt. Defiance tremendous. (Still, the Pratt Lake trail, Hike 86, gets to the same places more sensibly.)

Drive Interstate 90 to Bandera Airfield Exit 45. Go off the freeway and under it, then straight ahead on road No. 9030. At a split in 1 mile go straight ahead on road No. 9031, signed "Mason Lake Way." At 3.8 miles from the freeway the road is blocked. Park here, elevation 2100 feet.

Ascend the abandoned road about ½ mile to the torrent of Mason Creek; 300 feet beyond, the sign often hidden by brush, find the Mason Lake trail, which starts out switchbacking upward, in fairly decent fashion—and then goes all to pieces. Beaten out by boots with rarely a helping ax or saw, the way goes nearly straight up. At about 1¼ miles the grade eases to cross the boulder field, the route marked (and often

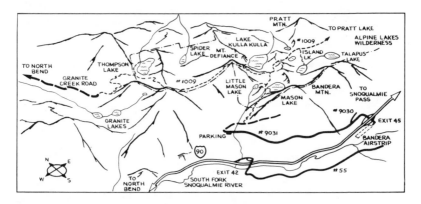

McClellan Butte and Interstate 90 from Mount Defiance

mismarked) by a confusion of cairns and plastic ribbons. A final bit of pleasant forest leads to Mason Lake, 4300 feet, 2½ miles. If camps are crowded here, try Little Mason Lake, reached by a swampy sidetrail that also passes a shallow pond. Within a mile are four other lakes. The Pratt Lake trail yields more.

For views, continue past Mason Lake, climbing 200 feet in ½ mile to a trail junction on the ridge crest between Mason Lake and Lake Kulla Kulla—and signs that suggest a week of explorations. Follow the ridge trail westward, ascending south slopes of Defiance. At 5200 feet, about 2 miles from the junction, traverse a large, steep meadow very near the 5400-foot summit, reached by a steep scramble up the west edge of the flower field. Look north over the Middle Fork Snoqualmie valley to Mt. Baker and Glacier Peak. Look south over the South Fork valley (with freeway) to Mt. Rainier and Mt. Adams.

The trail continues along the ridge, drops to Thompson Lake, then climbs over a spur to the ridgetop-to-creek-to ridgetop clearcuts of Granite Creek. If a hiker can arrange for a pickup on the Middle Fork Snoqualmie road, a one-way trip is possible.

| Bandera Viewpoint road | Old: 2218 | Old: 2218A |
| | New: 9030 | New: 9031 |

Island Lake from Bandera Mountain

SOUTH FORK SNOQUALMIE RIVER
Unprotected area

90 BANDERA MOUNTAIN

Round trip 7 miles
Hiking time 6 hours
High point 5240 feet
Elevation gain 2800 feet

Hikable mid-May through
October
One day
USGS Bandera

Though there is no real trail, just a boot-beaten track and follow-your-nose scramble, Bandera offers the easiest-to-reach summit panoramas in the Snoqualmie area, with superb views to the valley and lowlands, into the Alpine Lakes Wilderness, and up and down the length of the Cascades. Because of the southwesterly exposure, snow melts off early; the ascent can be made when trails to nearby peaks are still buried in winter white.

In the summer of 1958 a fire started by loggers swept Bandera to timberline. Long before that, in the past century, the upper slopes were burned (probably by nature's lightning, not by man's carelessness) and forest has not yet begun to come back. Thus the entire ascent is in the open and can be hot. To compensate, scenery is continuous every step of the way.

Drive to where road No. 9031 is blocked (Hike 89), elevation 2100 feet.

Walk the abandoned road, passing the Mason Lake trail, 1½ miles to the end. There's a creek here, and no water above.

Begin by scrambling uphill hear the creek, on boot-built tread, a short bit to a bulldozer track. Go rightward up the road a few hundred feet to a point where green timber at the margin of the burn is very close above. Climb the bank (where others obviously have done so) and a few yards of sparse brush to the edge of timber and there intersect the path hacked out by the fire fighters of 1958.

Ascend the rude, steep tread with hands and feet to the upper limit of the burn, then follow any of the paths directly upward, first over and around downed logs, then in low greenery of small shrubs and beargrass. Admire picturesque bleached snags from the 19th-century blaze. Off to the left, see a lichen-gray granite talus; listen for marmots whistling there.

The ridge crest is attained at around 4700 feet; immediately below on the far side is Mason Lake. The ridge is a good turnaround point for those who've had enough; the views are nearly as broad as those from the summit. The route to here often melts free of snow in early May.

Climb east on the crest through subalpine trees, then scramble granite boulders up a step in the ridge to the first summit, 5150 feet, and down-and-up a bit farther to the highest summit, 5240 feet. Look north to lakes in forest bowls below and far away to Glacier Peak and Mt. Baker, north-easterly to Snoqualmie peaks, south down to the highway and beyond to omnipresent Rainier, and west past the portal peaks of Washington and Defiance to lowlands. Civilization is near, but also wilderness.

Bandera Viewpoint road   Old: 2218
                         New: 9030

Mason Lake way   Old: 2218A
                  New: 9030

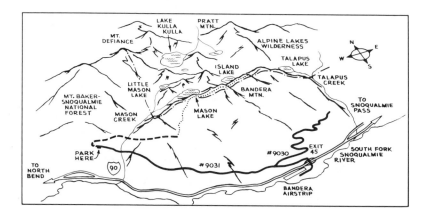

91   TAYLOR RIVER– NORDRUM LAKE

Round trip to Big Creek 10 miles
Hiking time 5 hours
High point 1700 feet
Elevation gain 500 feet
Hikable June through October
One day or backpack
USGS Mt. Si and Snoqualmie
    Lake

Round trip to Nordrum Lake 18
    miles
Allow 2 days
High point 3700 feet
Elevation gain 2500 feet
Hikable late July through
    mid-September

An abandoned logging road, now dwindled to an easy-strolling foot-road, and a rough and brushy and slippery and very steep scramble-trail combine to provide a varied experience of forest and rockslide, river and waterfall and subalpine lake. The road-trail is superb for spring and early summer when highlands are miserably white. The lake is the takeoff for some of the lonesome country in the Alpine Lakes Wilderness.

Drive Interstate 90 east from North Bend, at Exit 34 go off on Edgewick Road, turn left past Ken's Truck Town, then right on Middle Fork Snoqualmie River road No. 56, which in 15.5 miles crosses the Taylor River bridge and turns sharply right, downstream, becoming road No. 5620. Proceed straight (left) .3 mile upstream to the road-end at Taylor River trailhead No. 1002, elevation 1200 feet.

The hike begins by crossing the Taylor River and heading upvalley on the old road, which in 1000 feet splits; stay right, following the river. The road-trail, which is closed to four-wheel vehicles and should be to all wheels but is not (not yet), can be noisy on summer weekends when the hot sun stirs up the racketeers. It ascends gently in shade of second-

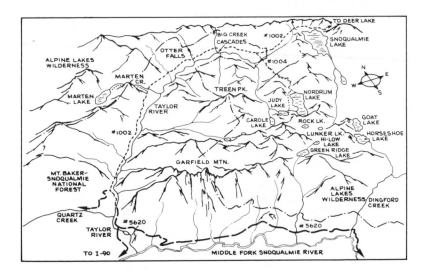

Nordrum Lake

growth and stands of virgin forest, passing numerous nice campsites. At
3 miles cross Marten Creek on a little wood bridge; look for a rude path
climbing to the falls. In another long mile pause to admire Otter Falls
and at 5 miles, 1700 feet, reach the granite cascades of Big Creek and a
heavy-duty concrete bridge, as anomalous as a helicopter in an alpine
meadow. Admire the white splash of water over clean granite, perhaps
stick a leg or a head in a pool, finish off the cherry tomatoes and granola
bars and turn for home.

Or continue. At 5¾ miles trail No. 1002 ascends left toward Snoqualmie, Deer, Bear, and Dorothy Lakes (Hike 2). In ¼ mile more the road
quits at 1800 feet and Nordrum Lake trail starts, 6 miles from the cars.

It's a rough start, crossing the river on logs, and gets rougher, aiming
straight at the sky up a staircase of rocks and roots that in early summer
doubles as a streambed. At 1½ miles (from the road trail) the way goes
over a creek frothing down granite and climbs onward, nearly overgrown
by ferns. At 2½ miles the path wanders casually westward beneath a
rockslide and ascends slippery granite slabs. The forest opens briefly to
views over the Taylor valley to Dog Mountain and lesser summits.

A short descent leads to Nordrum Lake, 4 miles, 3670 feet. To the left
is one small camp. For better sites on the west shore round the base of a
cliffy hillside, passing an old cabin site.

The lake is the takeoff for back-country roaming. A rough, boot-beaten
path weaves through basins and over saddles to Rock Lake, Lunker
Lake, Hi-Low Lake, Green Ridge Lake, and pretty little Quartz Lake.

Middle Fork road   Old: 2445
                    New: 56

HESTER LAKE

Round trip 12 miles
Hiking time 7 hours
High point 3886 feet
Elevation gain 2500 feet

Hikable July through October
One day or backpack
USGS Snoqualmie Lake

The Dingford Creek trail is a parade of fishing poles, each of the thousands expecting to haul in a share of the hundreds of poor little tame trout planted by man and wishing they'd never left the hatchery. Of the two main fish markets, Myrtle Lake (Hike 93) has lots of scenery and people, Hester some scenery and a bit of solitude. The trout-free ridges are lonesome.

Drive the Middle Fork road 15.5 miles, to the Taylor River bridge (Hike 91), and stay on it (the No. changing from 56 to 5620) another 6 miles to Dingford Creek trail No. 1005, elevation 1400 feet.

The trail switchbacks steeply 1 mile up sizable second-growth forest dating from the logging operation a half-century ago, enters the Alpine Lakes Wilderness, and at 1¼ miles eases the grade in cool virgin forest of tall, old Douglas fir and hemlock, going along constantly close to the tumble and roar of Dingford Creek. At about 2 miles, 2600 feet, are a ford of Goat Creek and an unmaintained fish-hunters' sidetrail climbing a rough 1 mile to Horseshoe Lake and Goat Lake.

At 3⅓ miles, 2900 feet, the trail splits. The left fork goes to super-popular Myrtle Lake. The right fork, to Hester, is in poor shape and will be allowed to stay that way for people wanting a chance to get away from people.

The rude path crosses Dingford Creek, passes a nice campsite, then ascends, moderately at first, in subalpine meadow-marshes and patches of trees, before heading straight uphill to Hester Lake, 6 miles, 3886 feet. The deep blue waters are set in a cirque gouged from 6500-foot Mt. Price; impressive cliffs rise from the shores but leave space for comfortable camps.

| Middle Fork road | Old: | 2445 | Beyond Taylor River | Old: | 241 |
| | New: | 56 | | New: | 5620 |

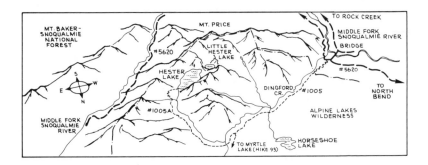

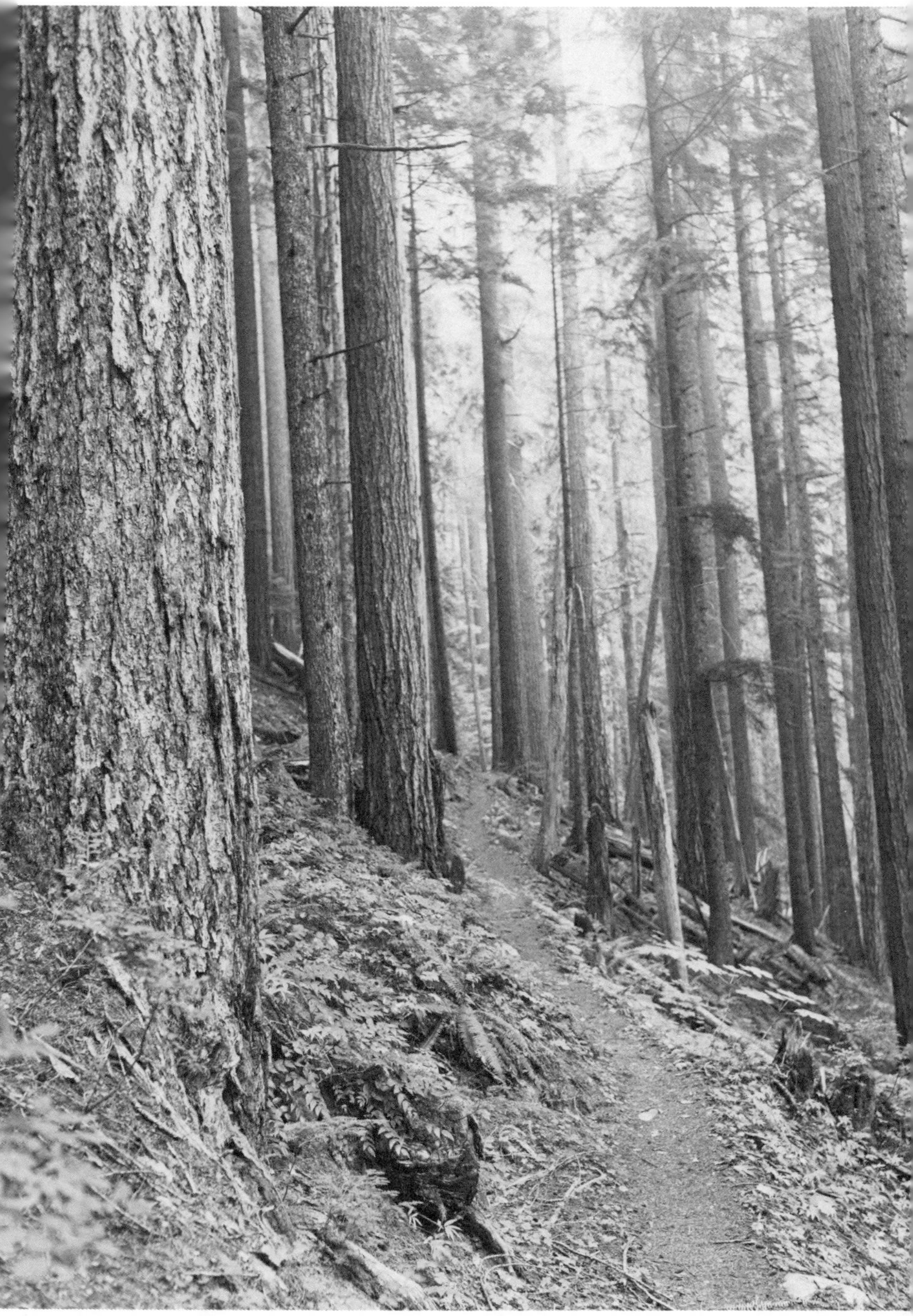

Dingford Creek trail

Myrtle Lake and Big Snow Mountain

93   MYRTLE LAKE

Round trip 14 miles
Hiking time 7 hours
High point 3777 feet
Elevation gain 2400 feet

Hikable July through October
One day or backpack
USGS Snoqualmie Lake and Big
    Snow Mountain

A thronged subalpine lake ringed by forest and heather gives a good look at 6680-foot Big Snow Mountain, monarch of the vicinity, and, for the doughty, intriguing explorations away from the crowds, up on the ridges where the wild boots go.

Drive to Dingford Creek trail No. 1005, elevation 1400 feet, and hike it 3⅓ miles to a split, 2900 feet (Hike 92).

The right fork goes to Hester Lake. Go left on Myrtle Lake trail No. 1005, making a short switchback and then a long upvalley traverse, ascending a moderate grade over a few rough spots and muddy stretches to the lake, 7 miles, 3777 feet. Campsites are on both sides of the outlet. For views of Big Snow Mountain take the boot-beaten path leftward around the south shore.

Boots can go where clouds can go. Turn right, over the outlet. The trail shrinks to a path and then, like the Cheshire cat, vanishes altogether in knee-deep brush crisscrossed by windfall. Cross Myrtle's inlet stream to the west side (the USGS incorrectly shows the trail staying on the east side) and proceed upvalley, the trail magically reappearing, quite good though unmaintained. The way switchbacks steeply, passing waterfalls, and at 1 mile from the cirque of Big Myrtle levels off in the upper cirque of Little Myrtle Lake, 4100 feet.

Switchbacks resume ½ mile to a 4500-foot pass at the head of the Miller River and the end of once-upon-a-time-built trail. For views out the Miller valley to Lake Dorothy drop a few feet down the northern slopes. Meager footpaths and game traces lead to lakelets probably without fish and thus possibly without people.

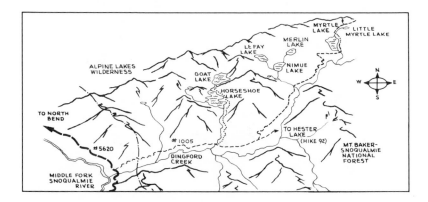

215

94 MIDDLE FORK SNOQUALMIE RIVER

One-way trip 6¼ miles
Hiking time 3 hours
High point 2200 feet
Elevation gain 800 feet

Hikable May through early
November
One day or backpack
USGS Snoqualmie Pass,
Snoqualmie Lake, Big Snow
Mountain

Within the memory of folks still nimbly ambling the back country a hiker setting out up the Middle Fork hoisted pack at North Bend. Then "lokie loggers" entered the valley with rails and spent a dozen-odd years clearcutting the floor of the glacial trough (and of Pratt River as well), climbing the valley walls as far as a high-line cable could skid logs to a landing. They obliterated most of the trail and caused much of the rest to be abandoned. It was replaced by the CCC Truck Road—built in the 1930s by one of the New Deal's best ideas, the Civilian Conservation Corps—to the Taylor River, and beyond there by a new foot route along the railroad grade. The upper stretch remained intact as the Cascade Crest Trail, another shining idea of the 1930s, but a substantial segment was relegated to the past when rerouting the Crest Trail via Gold Creek was completed in the 1970s.

Now, however, the Forest Service (constantly nagged by hikers who remind that "multiple use" has converted virtually all low-elevation trails to logging roads and that the long, wide, bottom of the magnificent Middle Fork valley, closest recreation area of such dimensions so near Puget Sound City, offers next to no quiet and peaceful recreation except roadside picnicking) plans to rebuild the trail—ultimately, one may hope, all the way from North Bend, there connecting it to a King County trail (open now, de facto) from Seattle's West Point, on the shores of Puget Sound. Part of the Middle Fork route is already walkable; however, since bridges wash out and may not be quickly replaced, before a hike call the Forest Service at North Bend.

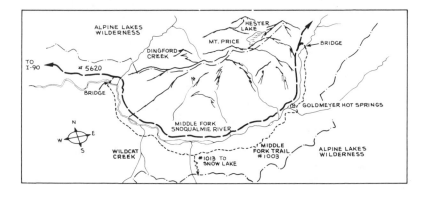

Middle Fork Snoqualmie River's upper trail bridge

Drive to the Dingford Creek trailhead, elevation 1400 feet (Hike 92). By late summer of 1986 this will be the lower trailhead for Middle Fork Snoqualmie trail No. 1003 and also Rock Creek trail No. 1013 (Hike 95).

For the upper trailhead, drive 4.5 miles farther upvalley and go right .4 mile (your car may request you to walk) on a very rough road to the end, elevation 2200 feet.

From the lower trailhead the way begins (or will) by crossing the Middle Fork on an airy, foot-only suspension bridge, no dancing allowed, and turning upvalley on a newly reopened section of old trail. The path climbs above the valley floor to sidehill through virgin forest of big, old Douglas fir and hemlock, dips to Wildcat Creek, reclimbs, dips to Rock Creek at 2 miles, 1520 feet, and passes an abandoned sidetrail that used to go over the river. Climb again, level out on an old logging railroad grade, and shortly pass the Rock Creek trail to Snow Lake. Formerly, the Cascade Crest Trail from Snoqualmie Pass descended Rock Creek and followed the Middle Fork to Dutch Miller Gap; you are now on that route. Proceed 2¾ miles in a tall-tree cathedral to the trail from Red Pass (Hike 83); this, too, formerly was the Cascade Crest Trail, until abandoned due to a hazardous snowbank that lingers much of the summer just below the summit.

In a short bit cross Burnt Boot Creek (on a bridge, one hopes, for it is a mighty tumble of loud water) to Goldmeyer Hot Springs, once a rustic spa where valetudinarians came to take the waters, and now, the Forest Service having failed to snap up the property when it could have been had for a song, a private campground. The public, however, has legal rights to walk through to the far side, where a log may be crossed to the road. Don't do it. The best is yet to come, 1½ miles beside the bellowing river, the forest the oldest, the mossiest, the greenest, the tallest, and at last on a handsome log bridge spanning the flood to the upper trailhead—which until the lower trailhead is finished is the place to start the hike. Why stop now? A few steps along the road puts you on the con-

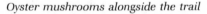

Oyster mushrooms alongside the trail

Middle fork Snoqualmie River

tinuation of the trail to Dutch Miller Gap (Hike 96).

To make a wilderness larger, one goes slower, putting away machines and wheels, traveling by muscles and feet. In years when the Taylor River blows away its wheel bridges and hikers shoulder packs there, the Alpine Lakes Wilderness is marvelously expanded, the hike to Dutch Miller Gap lengthened by a day or two. Permanent closure of the Middle Fork road at that point is the goal. Meanwhile, by starting at Dingford Creek, hikers can add half a day to their Dutch Miller experience. If the Forest Service keeps rebuilding the trail, eventually trips can begin at North Bend, recouping the losses of two-thirds of a century. This, not building more roads, is true progress.

MIDDLE FORK SNOQUALMIE RIVER
Alpine Lakes Wilderness

95 ROCK CREEK – SNOW LAKE

Round trip to Snow Lake 15 miles
Hiking time 9 hours
High point 4100 feet
Elevation gain 2800 feet

Hikable mid-July through
    September
One day or backpack
USGS Snoqualmie Lake and
    Snoqualmie Pass

Since the Cascade Crest Trail moved to Gold Creek to become the
Pacific Crest Trail, this portion of the old route has gotten so lonesome

Snow Lake

that half the tread is soft moss. To be sure, the brush has grown up too, one particular half-mile may be real misery, and some of the rockslides are less than pleasant. But you'll have have Rock Creek to keep you company, 1200 vertical feet of cascades and falls spilling from Snow Lake, and no people to keep you company until the lake. Worth it. Compared to the approach used by the masses from Snoqualmie Pass, this is 5½ miles longer and gains 1100 feet more elevation.

The Rock Creek trail lies across the Middle Fork Snoqualmie River from the road and as of 1985 there is no guaranteed easy way over, though at 2.2 miles on the road upvalley from Dingford Creek one may spot a large log that served as a bridge before the river changed course, and one may find a nearby logjam that can be crossed to the trail, but that's chancy business. The trip therefore will be described as it will be started the summer of 1986, when a new bridge is in place.

Drive to Dingford Creek trailhead, elevation 1400 feet, and hike Middle Fork Snoqualmie River trail No. 1003 (Hike 94) for 2 miles to the crossing of Rock Creek (passing the old Rock Creek trail that was abandoned because the Middle Fork Snoqualmie River kept changing course, leaving bridges stranded over dry channels). The trail turns uphill, paralleling Rock Creek, then levels off on an old railroad grade. At 2½ miles turn right on Rock Creek trail No. 1013, elevation 1650 feet.

At 3½ miles climb to views out the Middle Fork valley to Yosemite-like granite walls of Garfield Mountain, at 4½ miles leave second-growth for virgin forest, and at 5½ miles look out windows to the Rock Creek headwall and the great waterfall. At 6 miles is the miserable brush-covered rockslide, ending at 6½ miles when the way climbs over a rocky rib to meet the Snow Lake trail, 7½ miles, 4100 feet. The lake is a short walk in either direction; if camping, turn right for the least-mobbed sites.

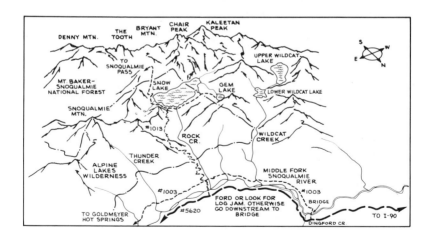

96 DUTCH MILLER GAP– LA BOHN GAP

Round trip to Dutch Miller Gap 15 miles
Allow 2–3 days
High point 5000 feet
Elevation gain 2000 feet
Hikable mid-July through October
USGS Big Snow Mountain and Mt. Daniel

Round trip to La Bohn Gap approximately 16 miles
High point 5600 feet
Elevation gain 2600 feet
Hikable late July through October

Hike a glorious valley of forests and meadows and waterfalls, rockslides and cliffs and jagged peaks, to wilderness headwaters of the Middle Fork Snoqualmie River. Then follow either the main trail to Dutch Miller Gap, named for an early prospector, or a way trail to La Bohn Gap, where he dug his holes in the ground.

Drive Middle Fork Snoqualmie River road to Dingford Creek (Hike 92) and 6 more miles to the road-end at Hardscrabble Creek, elevation 3000 feet.

The trail enters forest and ascends gently with ups and downs, passing a riverbank camp at 1½ miles.

The transition from low country to high is abrupt: at about 4 miles the trail switchbacks up a step in the valley, going by a splendid cataract of the river, and at the top emerges into heather, grass, flowers, large talus slopes, and views of craggy peaks. The way is flat and frequently marshy and muddy to 6 miles, where the river is so wide and slow and meandering as almost to be a lake, surrounded by a broad meadow. Here, at superbly scenic Pedro Camp, 4100 feet, the trail crosses a branch of the river on a bridge; shortly beyond prowl around to find remnants of an old miner's cabin (Dutch Miller's?).

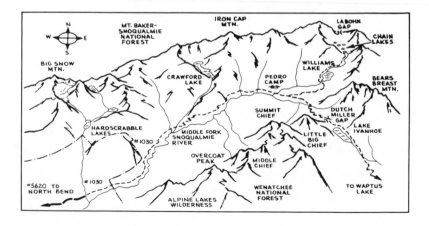

Williams Lake and Little Big Chief Mountain

The way goes moderately upward in heather and alpine trees another ½ mile to a junction with the Williams Lake–La Bohn Gap trail, an easy ¾ mile to the heather-fringed lake.

For the main event, follow tread a long mile or so and then climb rockslides and/or snowfields to a magnificent basin of cold little tarns set in granite bowls, of flower patches and waterfalls, and of the mineral outcroppings and diggings and garbage of Dutch Miller's old mine—and of his contemporary successors. Climb a bit more to the 5600-foot crest of La Bohn Gap (2 miles from the junction) and more tarns and views of Bears Breast Mountain and down to Necklace Valley (Hike 5). Experienced roamers can walk to panoramas from 6585-foot La Bohn Peak west of the gap or make a more difficult scramble to the summit of 7492-foot Mt. Hinman. Many delightful camps in the basin and in the gap.

One-half mile from the Williams Lake junction the main valley trail fords the river and ascends between the walls of Bears Breast and Little Big Chief, with grand views of Little Big Chief, Summit Chief, Middle Chief, and Overcoat, to the gardens of Dutch Miller Gap, 7½ miles, 5000 feet. Look immediately below to Lake Ivanhoe and out the valley east to Waptus Lake. Look westerly back down the long Snoqualmie valley. The trail drops ½ mile to rock-shored Ivanhoe, 4652 feet, at the foot of the cliffs of Bears Breast. Good camps by the lake. The trail continues down to Waptus Lake and the Cle Elum River (Hike 67).

| Middle Fork road | Old: | 2445 | Beyond Taylor River | Old: | 241 |
| | New: | 56 | | New: | 5620 |

97 MOUNT SI

**Round trip to Haystack Basin 8
  miles**
Hiking time 8 hours
High point 3600 feet
Elevation gain 3100 feet
Hikable April through November

One day
**USGS on the corner of Mt. Si,
  Snoqualmie, North Bend,
  Bandera**

Climb steeply to the top of a scarp rising high above lowlands at the west edge of the Cascades. Look down to the Snoqualmie River meandering by the towns of North Bend and Snoqualmie and through green farms. If the smog isn't too thick, look west to Seattle and Puget Sound and the Olympic Mountains.

Si is a striking landmark at the gateway to the Cascades and is close to the city and therefore is perhaps the most heavily traveled peak in the state. Mountaineers use the trail for conditioning. Scouts come in troops, and families with little children, and elderly folk and young lovers and lone roamers—a cross-section of humanity (in fact, about 10,000 hikers a year) may be encountered on a typical Sunday.

By May of normal years the way is entirely clear of snow. Sometimes the mountain is briefly bare even in midwinter, and the trail usually can be hiked to high viewpoints in any month.

Drive Interstate 90 to North Bend, take Exit 31 into town, and continue east on North Bend Way, the old route of Interstate 90. Exactly 1 mile from the east edge of town turn left on 432nd S.E. (Mt. Si Road) and cross the Middle Fork Snoqualmie River. Turn right at the first intersec-

North Bend at night from Mount Si

tion. Drive 2.5 miles to a parking lot for 175 cars, a picnic area, and the trailhead, elevation 650 feet. The trail is signed for hikers only.

The first ½ mile is in alders, then second-growth firs 60 to 70 years old—except for a 1976 clearcut. At 1 mile is a vista point on a big rock alongside the trail. At 1¾ miles enter Snag Flat, covered by a mixture of old snags and huge fir trees, some 8 feet in diameter, that survived the fires. Water here about 200 feet off the main trail on a spur going ½ mile to a viewpoint.

The trees get smaller but views are scarce until the old trail is intersected at 3 miles, just below the ridge, a mile from the top. The way follows a rocky shoulder with broad panoramas to Haystack Basin, at the foot of the cliffs of the final peak. The Department of Natural Resources, which relocated the trailhead and built the new path after the old one was partially obliterated by logging operations, has installed pit toilets and primitive campsites. However, there is no water after the last snow melts, usually in May, so carry enough for cooking or else hike up after dinner, enjoy the night on top—thousands of lights below and millions of stars above—and return to the car for breakfast. There are no other camps on the route.

The summit of the Haystack, elevation 4167 feet, may be climbed by scrambling up a steep, loose-rock gully on the northeast side of the basin, but the ascent is not recommended: it is a bit difficult, slippery in wet weather, and quite hazardous. The summit view is only slightly better than that from the basin.

Although too isolated by miles of clearcuts to be considered for the Alpine Lakes Wilderness, part of the mountain has been designated by the state legislature as the Mt. Si Preservation Area. The Department of Natural Resources is developing a management plan that will make provision for more hiking trails while leaving certain cliff-guarded enclaves undisturbed and superwild for mountain goats and other creatures. Conservationists, meanwhile, are proposing both enlargement of the too-small designated area, closure of certain high-elevation logging roads presently used as illegal accesses by motorcycles, and ultimate construction of a ridge trail from Si to Teneriffe to Green to Bessemer to Quartz—a highline wildland entry to the Alpine Lakes Wilderness.

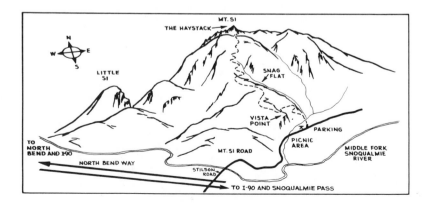

98   BARE MOUNTAIN

Round trip 8 miles	**Hikable late June through**
Hiking time 6 hours	**October**
High point 5353 feet	**One day**
Elevation gain 3250 feet	**USGS Mt. Si and Grotto**

A lonesome trail up a green hillside to a former fire lookout with panoramic views north to Mt. Baker and south to Mt. Rainier and west to the Olympics. So little-walked is the path that the tread is grown up in moss and grass—and may be lost under a canopy of flowers and bracken.

Drive Interstate 90 to North Bend, take Exit 31 into town and onto the main street, the former highway. Go two blocks east of the stoplight and turn north on Ballaratt Street, which leads to North Fork Country Road. At 4 miles from North Bend is a Y; take the left, uphill, signed "Lake Hancock." In 7.5 miles pass the Lake Hancock junction and proceed onward. At about 21 miles enter national forest, the road now becoming Lennox Creek road No. 57. At the boundary the road forks; keep right, crossing Lennox Creek. At 23 miles from North Bend (what with all the chuckholes on the country segment, allow an hour for the drive) is the trailhead, signed "Bare Mountain trail No. 1037." Park here, elevation 2100 feet.

The first 2 miles follow an abandoned mining road, crossing Bear Creek on a wide bridge near a beautiful pool. (*Note*: It's "Bare" Mountain and "Bear" Creek. Were they named for two different reasons?) In ¼ mile the way recrosses the creek on a footbridge, enters the Alpine Lakes Wilderness, and climbs another ¼ mile to a large meadow covered with waist-high bracken. Find the trail with your feet—but watch out for hidden holes! At about 2 miles from the car may be a small white post obscurely marking a junction, 3650 feet. Go left. (The right fork dead-ends at an old mining claim. If after crossing the large meadow you enter forest, you are ¼ mile beyond the junction on this, the wrong way.)

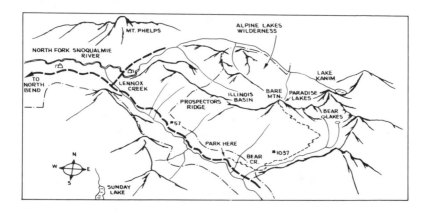

Glacier Peak from Bare Mountain

The left (correct) fork sets out from the junction so deep under ferns the boots can feel it but the eyes can't see it. Eventually, though, the path emerges in the open and after gaining 1700 feet in 46 switchbacks attains the 5353-foot summit.

All that remains of the lookout cabin, which was removed in 1973, is broken glass, rusting cables—and a grand view.

The three Paradise Lakes sparkle below, a tempting 1000-foot dive; due to formidable cliffs, this seems the only practical way to get there from here.

Lennox Creek road   Old: 250
                     New: 57

Anderson Lake, snow-covered in late June; Treen Peak (left) *and Garfield Mountain* (center)

NORTH FORK SNOQUALMIE RIVER
Alpine Lakes Wilderness

99   LENNOX CREEK

Round trip to Anderson Lake 7¼ miles
Hiking time 5 hours
High point 4600 feet
Elevation gain 1900 feet in, 400 feet out

Hikable July through early November
One day or backpack
USGS Mt. Si and Snoqualmie Lake

Waterfalls, broad slopes of heather meadows, views of peaks and valleys, and a quiet lake—all a little-traveled portion of the Cascades. After lying in limbo for many years, this trail was reopened in 1970, hikers began to discover the beauties of the North Fork Snoqualmie country, and as a consequence the Alpine Lakes Wilderness boundaries were drawn to preserve some of them.

Drive about 21 miles from North Bend to the boundary of Mt. Baker–Snoqualmie National Forest and keep right at the fork here (Hike 98). From the boundary drive 4 miles to two small bridges over island-divided channels of Lennox Creek. About .2 mile farther is a fork; keep right on road No. (5700)210, heading up Cougar Creek drainage a short, switchbacking mile to the road-end at a hogback in a clearcut, elevation 2700 feet.

The trail starts steeply up the hogback on a bulldozer track, in less than ¼ mile going from logged barrens into forest and passing a miner's cabin. Now the way contours the east side of Dog Mountain, traversing shoulders of a large avalanche chute. At about 2 miles the route enters a land of heather laced by numerous creeklets. Directly below the meadows and a bit hard to see is the spectacular waterfall of one of the tributaries of Lennox Creek.

At about 3¼ miles, 4600 feet, the trail gains a wooded saddle in the ridge. Enjoy the views down to Taylor River and across the valley to Treen Peak and a most unfamiliar aspect of Garfield Mountain.

From the saddle the trail switchbacks down 400 feet in a rough ½ mile to little Anderson Lake, surrounded by patches of heather and lots of trees. Camping is nice and quite private but wood is scarce.

Lennox Creek road   Old: 250   Cougar Creek road   Old: 250B
                   New: 57   New: (5700)210

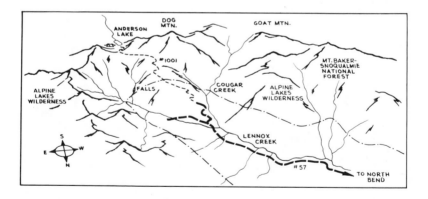

IOO PACIFIC CREST TRAIL

One-way trip between Snoqualmie Pass and Stevens Pass 67 miles
Allow 5 days minimum
High point 5800 feet
Elevation gain about 10,600 feet

Hikable mid-July through mid-September
USGS Snoqualmie Pass, Big Snow Mountain, Mt. Daniel, The Cradle, Scenic, Stevens Pass

The segment of the Mexico–to–Canada Pacific Crest National Scenic Trail between Snoqualmie Pass and Stevens Pass traverses the complete south–north width of the Alpine Lakes Wilderness, sampling superb scenery of the Cascade Crest, highland flower gardens, deep-shadow virgin forests, lakes, waterfalls, the peace that surpasseth, all on a well-graded trail with numerous choice camps and a lifetime of sidetrips.

Close to Puget Sound City and population centers of Central Washington as it is, and drawing wilderness lovers from across the nation, the trail is among the most popular in America. To guard the fragile

Bears Breast Mountain and Mount Hinman from Pacific Crest Trail

meadows, lakeshores, and streambanks from excessive wear and tear hikers must be gentle, camping only in designated, established sites or well away (say, ¼ mile or more) from the trail, and faithfully observing the principles of no-trace camping.

The following is a summary of the route; for more detail and exact mileage logs consult the Forest Service map, available at any office. From Stevens Pass the trail continues 185 miles north to Allison Pass in Canada (see *100 Hikes in the North Cascades*), and from Snoqualmie Pass, 97 miles south to the Columbia River (see *100 Hikes in the South Cascades and Olympics*).

Obviously, the trip can be done in either direction and is described here

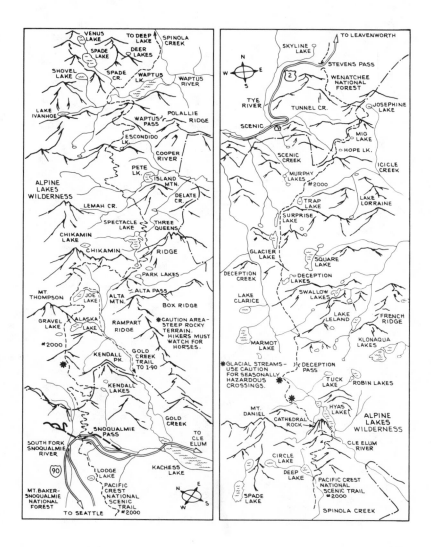

Alaska Lake from Pacific Crest Trail

from south to north for no particular reason. A favorite strategy is to do it one way, having some benefactor provide the drop off and pickup. An important reason hikers are drawn from great distances is the availability of public transportation at both ends of the trail, permitting a group (say) to fly from Detroit to Seattle, catch a bus to one pass or another, catch another bus back to Seattle, and fly home; leaving the driving to them.

Drive Interstate 90 east to Snoqualmie Pass, go off on Exit 52, cross under the freeway, and on the first right proceed uphill to the Pacific Crest Trail No. 2000 parking area, elevation somewhat above 3000 feet.

The way climbs high on Kendall Peak (Hike 82) and ridge-runs meadows to Ridge Lake and the first campsites, 6 miles. (*Note:* Snow lingering late on the Kendall Katwalk may force through-hikers to detour from or to Snoqualmie Pass via Joe Lake and Gold Creek, Hike 80.) It makes a great near-contouring swing around the head of Gold Creek's glacial trough, passing above Alaska and Joe Lakes (designated camps in the saddle above the latter cirque), sidehilling garden slopes of Alaska and Huckleberry Mountains and Chikamin Peak, and drops to the next designated camps at 15 miles, on a meadow ridge above Park Lakes.

Ascend parkland to the grand views from Spectacle Point (Hike 82) on a shoulder of Three Queens Mountain and drop to Spectacle Lake junction (Hike 62), 17 miles; camps are abundant at the lake and along the creek. Continue mainly downhill 4 miles to the next camp at the crossing of Lemah Creek. Other camps are near the Pete Lake trail junction, at the start of switchbacks ascending a shoulder of Summit Chief Mountain, and before and after Escondido Ridge Tarns, 27 miles. Pass Escondido Lake at 27½ miles, the Waptus Burn trail, another camp, and drop to cross the Waptus River, 32 miles. Round Waptus Lake to an excellent camp at Spade Lake trail and a split in the trail; either climb high across open-forested slopes or round the lakeshore to many popular camps (Hikes 67 and 68); the paths rejoin on the long ascent of Spinola Creek, passing more camps, to Deep Lake (Hike 75), 39 miles.

Switchback up from the deep cirque to Cathedral Pass, 42½ miles, and roll down and up slopes of Cathedral Rock and Mt. Daniel to Deception Pass (Hike 73), 47½ miles. (**Note:** Two tumbling streams below Daniel are so hazardous in early-summer snowmelt and fall cloudbursts that hikers often are forced to detour from Cathedral Pass to Deception Pass via Squaw Lake and Hyas Lake; watch for warning signs at the junctions.) Camps are about a mile west of Deception Pass on the Marmot Lake trail (Hike 76).

Swing on the near-level around the head of Deception Creek to Deception Lakes (Hike 9) and camps, climb the side of Surprise Mountain to Pieper Pass, and drop to Glacier Lake, 54¼ miles. Ascend forest to a parkland pass, drop to Trap Lake, traverse a meandering ridge, and drop to limited camps in the huckleberry meadows of Hope Lake and then Mig Lake (Hike 10). Descend to a wooded pass, regain the ridge, and pass near Swimming Deer Lake (Hike 11), 62½ miles. Swing around the cirque above Josephine Lake, through a saddle, and down to Lake Susan Jane and the last (first) camps; proceed out of the Alpine Lakes Wilderness and under power lines of upper Mill Creek, then down the ski area to the trailhead parking area at Stevens Pass, 67 miles.

STILL MORE HIKES
IN THE ALPINE LAKES

Though this book describes major trails in the Cascades from Snoqualmie Pass to Stevens Pass, countless other pathways—many abandoned and all but forgotten—and easy-walking off-trail routes offer pristinity and solitude. Some 55-odd are noted below, and the list is far from exhaustive. As the major trails grow more thronged, the lesser become more attractive; as even the lesser obtain a considerable population, the brush begins to look good. Thanks to most hikers being content to stay safely and sanely on well-maintained tread, as little as ¼ mile from the likes of Interstate 2000, the Pacific Crest Freeway, may suffice to escape the thud of boots, the roar of backpacker stoves, and the crunching of freeze-dried shrimp and the slurping of portable soup. To take the following hikes, obtain the appropriate maps and let your imagination and feet run wild.

SKYKOMISH

West Fork Miller River: An abandoned road, now a pleasant forest trail beside the stream. (See *Footsore 2*.)

NASON CREEK

Lanham Lake trail No. 1589: 1¾ miles to lake under cliffs of Jim Hill Mountain. Crosses powerline road and parallels a logging road ½ mile. (Closed to bikes and horses.)

Lake Grace trail No. 1578: 1½ miles to a high alpine lake below Snowgrass Mountain. Trail starts from Wildhorse trail No. 1592 (Hike 14), ¾ mile below Frosty Pass. Trail is no longer maintained.

Glacier Creek trail No. 1573: 2 miles from North Fork Chiwaukum Creek (Hike 18) to a beautiful cirque. Trail is not maintained.

ICICLE CREEK

Jack Creek trail No. 1558: 11½ miles along forested Jack Creek to meadows and Stuart Pass.

Meadow Creek trail No. 1559: A long, forested hike from the Jack Creek trail No. 1558 to Scatter Creek Pass and Paddy-Go-Easy Pass. Easier approach from Cle Elum River (Hikes 43 and 44).

Solomon Creek trail No. 1593: 3¼-mile trail from Jack Creek trail to Van Epps Pass jeep road.

Sylvester Lake: 3½-mile fishermen route climbing steeply from Icicle Creek road to a beautiful alpine lake below Grindstone Mountain.

MISSION CREEK

Magnet Creek trail No. 1206: 3-mile connector between US 97 and Tiptop—Mt. Lillian trail No. 1204.

Squilchuck trail No. 1200: 2-mile hike through alpine forest. Access to Clara and Marion Lakes.

Falls Creek trail No. 1216: 3-mile trail, accessing Negro Creek Basin, Navaho Peak, and Three Brothers from Ingalls Creek trail (Hike 43).

Cascade Creek trail No. 1217: 3-mile trail connecting Stafford Creek to Ingalls Creek trail No. 1215.

Hardscrabble–Forth Creek trail: 2–4-day loop trip starting from Beverly–Turnpike trail or Ingalls Creek trail (Hikes 51 and 43).

Hansel Creek Ridge and return to Ingalls Creek; abandoned trail.

Negro Creek Basin trail No. 1210: This quiet, rarely visited area may be reached by trail from Ingalls Creek or by walking from North Shaser Creek. Forest Service plans to develop an ORV park here.

Three Brothers Mountain trail No. 1211: Steep trail to scenic old lookout site. Excellent views. Access same as Negro Creek Basin trail (above).

SWAUK PASS AREA (All below are open to motorbikes unless otherwise noted.)

Teanaway Ridge trail No. 1351A: Beginning at Red Top Mountain, crossing road No. 9702, meeting Iron-Bear Creek trail at 4½ miles and Blewett Summit trail at 7 miles (Hikes 47 and 46).

Tronsen Meadow trail No. 1205: 1½ miles between road No. (7240)411 in Tronsen Meadow and road No. 9712 in Upper Haney Meadow.

Ridge trail No. 1352: 4 miles from road No. 213 to Table Mountain road No. 3500. Trail follows ridge between First Creek and Boulder Creek. Some 4×4 use.

Regan trail No. 1354: 4¼-mile trail over Basalt Bluff with several viewpoints over Naneum Creek. To reach Regan trail take Nealy Creek trail No. 1370, then Naneum–Wilson trail No. 1371.

Snowshoe Ridge trail No. 1368: 2½-mile trail following open areas along ridge from road No. 3507 to Table Mountain road No. 35.

Nealy Creek trail No. 1370: 3¼-mile trail from Table Mountain road No. 35 to forest boundary. Trail poorly defined in open areas, closed to motorized travel.

Naneum–Wilson trail No. 1371: 6½-mile trail mainly in timber. Access from Table Mountain road No. 35.

Drop Creek trail No. 1371A: Access trail from road No. 35 to Naneum–Wilson trail No. 1371.

Owl Creek trail No. 1371B: 1¾-mile access from Table Mountain road No. 35 to Naneum–Wilson trail No. 1371.

First Creek trail No. 1374: 4¼ mile-trail used as a stock driveway from the Green Canyon road to Ridge trail No. 1352.

Wilson Creek trail No. 1387: 5 miles from Table Mountain road No. 2008 to the forest boundary.

Naneum Meadow trail No. 1389: 3½-mile trail from Table Mountain road No. 35, over upper Owl Creek, to Naneum Meadow (Hike 45).

TEANAWAY RIVER AREA (All below are open to motorbikes unless otherwise noted.)

West Fork Teanaway River trail No. 1353: 9½-mile trail from road No. 113 up the West Fork Teanaway River to Jolly Mountain trail No. 1307. Several difficult river crossings.

Middle Fork Teanaway River trail No. 1393: Follow an old wagon road along the Middle Fork from road No. 113 for 12 miles to the head of the valley and Paris Creek trail No. 1393. Numerous river crossings, no bridges.

Jolly Creek trail No. 1355: 4 mile-access from forested Middle Fork Teanaway trail No. 1393 to open meadows of Jolly Mountain trail No. 1307.

Way Creek trail No. 1235: Steep 1½-mile descent from Jungle Creek road No. 9701 to Middle Fork Teanaway River trail No. 1393. Way Creek access bypasses seven crossings of the Middle Fork River. Trail not maintained.

Jungle Creek trail No. 1383A: 4½-mile trail from Jungle Creek road No. 218 over a forested ridge to the Johnson Creek trail. Trailhead is difficult to locate.

Standup trail No. 1369: 5.9-mile climb to views of Stuart Range, joining with trail No. 1391A (Hike 52) below Earl Peak and ending at Stafford Creek trail No. 1359 (Hike 50) 1 mile from County Line trail No. 1210 (Hike 54). Closed to motorized vehicles.

Gallagher trail No. 1335: 4-mile jeep trail to mining claim and south to Boulder Creek, Jolly Mountain, and Sasse Mountain.

CLE ELUM RIVER

Domerie Peak trail No. 1308: Scenic 7-mile hike from road No. 4903-201 over Domerie Peak, Mt. Baldy, and Thomas Peak to the side of South Peak in the French Cabin Mountains. Limited water, but good views of Cle Elum Lake and Mt. Rainier.

Silver Creek Tie trail No. 1308A: 2½-mile connector between Domerie Peak trail No. 1308 and Kachess Ridge trail No. 1315 (Hike 60).

Sasse Mountain trail No. 1340: 9-mile sheep driveway along ridge tops from Hex Mountain to Jolly Mountain. Starts from road No. 4305-116, ends at trail No. 1330.

Hex Mountain trail No. 1343: Steady 1½-mile climb from road No. 116 to the open summit of Hex Mountain and Sasse Mountain trail No. 1340.

Red Mountain trail No. 1330: 7 miles long, connecting with the Kachess Ridge trail a mile short of Thorp Mountain Lookout (Hike 61). Alternate access to Red Mountain possible off spur road from Cooper Pass; abandoned trail follows ridge to meet trail No. 1330.

Trail Creek trail No. 1322: 4¾-mile trail from Cathedral Rock trail No. 1345 to Waptus River trail No. 1310, where the river must be forded.

Michael Lake trail No. 1336: Sidetrip from the Trail Creek trail No. 1322 for 6½ miles, past Michael Lake to Lake Terrance. Best reached from the Fish Lake end.

Paris Creek trail No. 1393: A short 8 miles to open basin where trail is difficult to follow. One could spend a week here without retracing path, since the trail joins the Teanaway, Jolly Mountain, and Boulder–DeRoux trails.

Boulder–DeRoux trail No. 1392: 4-mile jeep trail connecting to the Paris Creek trail and others.

Fortune Creek–Van Epps Pass trail No. 1544: Jeep "trail" to pass, and at 2½ miles, to old mining camp. Trail continues, very obscure, to Solomon Creek trail.

Fortune Creek spur trail No. 2342: Jeep trail from Van Epps Pass.

SOUTH FORK SNOQUALMIE RIVER

Guye Peak: Rough trail from Alpental ski area to saddle between Guye Peak and Snoqualmie Mountain.

MIDDLE FORK SNOQUALMIE RIVER

Mt. Teneriffe: 7 miles up a jeep road from valley and then ¾-mile trail to summit (see *Footsore 2*).

Granite Creek: Gated road and fishermen's path to Granite Lakes and Lake Thompson and connection with Defiance trail No. 1007 (see *Footsore 2*).

Lake Thompson: from Granite Creek road and trail.

Pratt River: 7 miles to Pratt Lake but until the bridge is built must first ford the Middle Fork Snoqualmie River.

Rainy Lake trail (not a trail) from Camp Brown: Route very difficult to find. 6 or 7 hours to lake.

Quartz Creek: Gated logging roads followed by a very difficult ¾-mile fishermen's trail to Blethan Lake.

Marten Lake trail No. 1006: 1 very brushy mile on rough fishermen's trail from the Taylor River road-trail.

INDEX